QUEEN B'S CONCOCTIONS

101 Adult
Liquorsicles and Cocktail Cups

Tina + Howard,

Enjoy creating these concoctions!
Happy Boozing!

Cheers
Jenny
5-30-14

ISBN: 1490410279
ISBN-13: 9781490410272

Library of Congress Control Number: 2013913515
CreateSpace Independent Publishing Platform
North Charleston, South Carolina

QUEEN B'S CONCOCTIONS

101 Adult
Liquorsicles and Cocktail Cups

Created by: Jenny Broderick

Photography by: Tino Langner

Photo Staging by:

Karen Adame of Designed to Perfection

DEDICATIONS

To my mom, Janet Spinner, who has always told me I should write a book!
I am sure this is not the type of book she was thinking of!

TO MY TASTE TESTERS

John Broderick, Lucy and Jim Mulholland,
Alfonso Loreto, Craig Risebury, Andy Henningsen,
Nick Henningsen and Karen Adame.
Thank you all for your support, taste buds and honest critiques!

TO MY CONCOCTION NAME HELPERS

Angie Lovejoy Knight, Karen Adame, Jim Spinner, Bob Spinner,
Dave Bigott and Dave Smuk. Thank you for getting your creative juices
flowing for some fun names!

TABLE OF CONTENTS

Top 10..xiii

Holiday Concoctions..xv

Introduction..xvii

Chapter 1 - The Laboratory 1

Chapter 2 - Removing the Molds. Storing and Serving Your Concoctions.........5

Chapter 3 - Infused Alcohol 9
- Berry Infused Vodka 14
- Lemon Infused Vodka 15
- Lime Infused Vodka 16
- Mango Infused Vodka 17
- Orange Infused Vodka...18
- Pineapple Infused Vodka..19
- Banana Rum...21
- Mango Rum..23
- Pineapple Rum..24

Chapter 4 - Champagne Concoctions...25
- Brandon's Cinnamon Cyclone..26
- Christmas Poinsettia...28
- Cupid's Arrow Champagne 31

- Paddy's Shamrock...35
- Passionate Peach Champagne 37
- Pomegranate Princess.......................................41
- The Morning After 43

Chapter 5 - Cream Concoctions. 45
- Arousing Almond 46
- Banana Hammock 47
- Baileys Bombshell..49
- Buttered Buns 51
- Candy Cane..52
- Captivating Caramel Tini.................................54
- Coconut Cupcake 55
- Cream of the Cropsicle 59
- Dolly Girl's Devil's Delight...............................61
- Her Majesty's Sinful Colada 63
- Island Hootch 65
- Kahlua Dream..66
- Kinky Key Lime 69
- Magical Moves Malted Milkshake....................73
- Marshmallow Elf..75
- Minty Fudge Madness.......................................77
- Moaning Minty Chip 79
- Mocha Freeze...80
- Monkey Business 83
- Nana's Nutella 85
- Nick the Nutty Nudist.......................................86
- Peach Whip 89
- Pleasing Pistachio Cloud 93
- Precarious Pumpkin Pie 95
- Queen B's Coconut Quest..................................97

- **Randy Russian** 98
- **Sassy Sassafras** 101
- **Skinny Dipper** 103
- **Sticky Caramel Apple** 107
- **Trade Winds** 109
- **White Chocolate Bunny** 111
- **Wicked Witches Brew** 113

Chapter 6 - Fruit Concoctions 115

- **Aaliyah's Amazing** 117
- **Alana's Almond** 119
- **American Flag** 121
- **Andy's Twisted Trucker** 124
- **Angela's Apricot** 126
- **Lori's Luscious Lemon** 128
- **Berry Pucker** 130
- **Blast Off Banana** 133
- **Blushing Baked Apple** 134
- **Bob's Blasted Berry** 137
- **Buzz's Beyond a Cosmo** 139
- **Captain's Booty** 141
- **Caribbean Casanova** 142
- **Caribbean Sunset** 143
- **Dreaming of a Daiquiri- Banana** 145
- **Dreaming of a Daiquiri- Blueberry** 145
- **Dreaming of a Daiquiri- Mango** 145
- **Dreaming of a Daiquiri- Orange** 146
- **Dreaming of a Daiquiri- Peach** 146
- **Dreaming of a Daiquiri- Pineapple** 147
- **Dreaming of a Daiquiri- Raspberry** 147

- **Dreaming of a Daiquiri- Strawberry**................................148
- **Dreaming of a Daiquiri- Traditional** 148
- **Easter Parade** 151
- **Gorgeous Grape**...153
- **Green Sandia**...157
- **Mexican Flag**...158
- **Green With Envy** 161
- **Island Breeze**...163
- **Jameson & Cranberry** 167
- **Jameson & Ginger Ale** 167
- **Jameson & Lemonade** 167
- **Jess's Pink Prescription** 169
- **Jimbo's Jamaican** 171
- **Kalena's Fiesta Sangria** 175
- **Long Day at the Office** 177
- **Luau Liftoff** 179
- **Luck of the Irish** 181
- **Lucy's Lip Smacker** 182
- **Ménage à Trois** 184
- **Mesmerizing Margarita-Mango** 185
- **Mesmerizing Margarita- Peach** 185
- **Mesmerizing Margarita- Strawberry** 187
- **Mesmerizing Margarita- Traditional** 187
- **Panty Raid**..189
- **Papa's Paradise** 191
- **Pink Coco**...195
- **Pirate's Brew**...196
- **Rainbow Rendezvous**...197
- **Raspberry Royalty** 203
- **Ravishing Red Grapefruit Martini**..............................205
- **Rock'n Raspberry**..206

- Ruby's Ringer 208
- Rapturous Rum 209
- Sarge's Salute 211
- Southern Orgasm 213
- Spinner's Special 217
- Suntan Slinger 218
- Tea'd Off Arnold 219
- Titillating Tropical Tahitian 220
- Voluptuous Melons 223
- Wacky Watermelon 225

Measures 226

Index 227

VOTED TOP 10!

1. Buttered Buns 51

2. Dolly Girl's Devil's Delight 61

3. Dreaming of a Daiquiri – Pineapple 147

4. Kinky Key Lime 69

5. Monkey Business 83

6. Nana's Nutella 85

7. Her Majesty's Sinful Colada 63

8. Skinny Dipper 103

9. Strawberry Margarita 187

10. Sticky Caramel Apple 107

HOLIDAY CONCOCTIONS

New Year's Eve   Pomegranate Princess 41
                             Passionate Peach Champagne 37

New Year's Day   The Morning After............................ 43

Valentine's Day   Cupid's Arrow Champagne 31
                             Raspberry Royalty 203

St Patrick's Day   Luck of the Irish 181
                             Paddy's Shamrock............................ 35

Easter   White Chocolate Bunny................. 111
                             Easter Parade 151

Cinco De Mayo   Green Sandia 157
                             Mexican Flag 158

4th of July/ Memorial Day American Flag 121
                             Sarge's Salute 211

Halloween   Wicked Witches Brew 113
                             Blushing Baked Apple 134
                             Sticky Caramel Apple 107

Thanksgiving   Brandon's Cinnamon Cyclone.......... 26
                             Precarious Pumpkin Pie 95

Christmas   Candy Cane 52
                             Christmas Poinsettia 28
                             Marshmallow Elf............................. 75

INTRODUCTION

COOL, FRESH AND REVITALIZING!

Remember the days when you were little and you would hear the ice cream man driving down your street ringing his bell? We would be so excited and would run to our mom and scream "ice cream man, ice cream man"! We wanted to run out with our money and get that frozen treat from him before he drove away. Then our mom would yell back "I have some in the freezer"! We would be so disappointed to be forced to have the ones in our freezer. Well, with these special concoctions in your freezer, you will not be disappointed again!

Just because we are all grown up does not mean we do not want a nice cold refreshing treat on those hot summer days! And if there is an extra "kick" in it then it's even better! These concoctions are great for BBQ's, parties, bridal and baby showers, girl's night in, dinner party desserts or even a special tasty treat after a stressful day. If you are having a bachelor or bachelorette party, these are fun with the adult themed molds. **(See page 3)**.

No time to make individual treats? You can make many of these recipes in one batch, freeze it in a container and then serve it like ice cream. The cream treats work best for this.

I have also made some of my own infused fruit vodkas and rums which really make a difference for a light refreshing frozen treat. (See chapter 4 for recipes)

WARNING!! Be sure to keep these away from the kids. All the treats do contain alcohol.

WARNING!! Do not eat these and drive.

CHAPTER 1

The Laboratory

The Laboratory

I have to admit that at times I felt like I was working in a chemistry lab while creating these recipes. I have done all the testing so it will be easy for you to make these fantastic frozen concoctions yourself. My first challenge was to get the treats to freeze. In general, the ratio of alcohol to sugar is what will prevent most home freezers from allowing alcohol to freeze. I include both alcohol and sugar in these recipes so I needed to come up with an emulsifier that would enable the process. I used Knox unflavored gelatin in all of the recipes to get them to freeze.

Kitchen Gadgets needed

You do not need to go out and buy a lot of kitchen gadgets to create these concoctions. You probably already have everything you need. Here is a list of necessary items: blender, pourable measuring cup, measuring spoons, bar shot glass showing various oz measures and Liquorsicle molds or dishes to freeze the recipes. Also, a small mesh sieve or a colander and cheese cloth to strain pureed fruits is suggested.

The smaller size molds work better for these recipes. Many companies have small molds for babies and children which are perfect. The majority of molds hold ¼ to ½ cup of liquid. Many of the molds come with their own sticks.

The fruit treats freeze well in the molds. The creamy treats freeze well in the molds and are also a great individual treat when frozen in a small ramekin type dish.

You can also use small disposable plastic bathroom cups and wood craft sticks. Do not use the colored sticks as the dye will seep into the treat. If you use the small plastic cups, let the treat freeze about 45-60 minutes before putting the sticks in or they may not stand up. You will also need to do this for molds without sticks. Many various containers in your kitchen can be used for the molds. Just remember you do not want anything too large as it will be difficult to eat it and the treats do contain alcohol so a little goes a long way!

I found inexpensive small plastic ramekin type cups and small condiment bowls at Wal-Mart by the kitchen items. These work great for the cream treats. Also, many party stores carry various sizes of small plastic decorative dessert cups which you can use.

Molds can be found at:

Amazon.com- under home and kitchen
Bed Bath & Beyond
Candyplus.net - **Warning: adult molds**
Casa.com - Tovolo Groovy Ice Pop Molds
Cheftools.com
Chocolatefantasies.com - **Warning: adult molds**
Ebay.com
Forsmallhands.com
Growingagreenfamily.com
Lehmans.com
Naturalmomgear.com - stainless steel molds
Naturemoms.com
Nawtythings.com - **Warning: adult molds**
Prairemoon.biz
Reuseit.com
Sears.com - Silicone Zone popsicle molds
Surlatable.com
Target
Thekitchn.com
Tupperware
Uncommongoods.com - fun different molds

Wal-Mart
Willams-Sonoma.com

Craft sticks can be found at:

Amazon.com
Discountschoolsupplies.com
Michaels Crafts
Hobby Lobby Crafts
Joanne Fabrics and Crafts
Wal-Mart craft section

CHAPTER 2

Removing the Molds. Storing and Serving Your Concoctions

Removing the Liqourscicle Molds

It is best to let the Liquorscicles freeze overnight to ensure they are completely frozen. Once your Liqoursicles are frozen you are ready to remove them from the molds.

You can either let the mold sit out for 3-4 minutes or run some tepid water over the mold while making sure that the water flow is below the rim of the mold. You can see through most of the molds that the mixture has released from the side of the mold. GENTLY, and with patience, pull on the stick so that the mixture will release from the mold and come out in one piece! If you notice the treat is not coming out in one piece, refreeze and try again in about 20-30 minutes. If your recipe calls for sprinkling nuts or sugars on the Liqoursicle, this is the time to do so. You are now ready to enjoy this delicious tasty treat!

Cocktail Cups

Once the cocktail cups are frozen through they are ready to serve. There is no need to remove the mixture from the cups. For best results let them sit out for 3-5 minutes so the texture is like ice cream.

Storing Your Concoctions

Liqoursicles- when you have removed them from the molds and are not going to eat them right away or are making a large batch at once for an event, you can store them for about 2 weeks in individual wax paper bags. If you cannot find wax paper bags, you can roll them in wax paper and put them in bunches in Ziploc type freezer bags. You must keep them sealed or ice crystals may start to form on the treats.

I found the wax paper bags on line as well as at neighborhood bakeries that make wedding cakes.

Cocktail Cups- The cocktail cups can also be stored in individual wax paper bags or wrapped in wax paper and put in Ziploc type freezer bags. They are good for 2 weeks before the ice crystals start to form.

Serving Your Concoctions

The Liqoursicles need to be eaten immediately once they are out of the freezer. If you are having a party you can serve them on a tub of ice, but again they must be eaten right away.

For best results in the cocktail cups, they are best served if taken out of the freezer and allowed to thaw for 3-5 minutes. If your recipe calls for adding whipped cream or other toppings, do this right before serving. You can get creative here as well with the extra toppings. Chocolate sprinkles, coconut, various ice cream toppings and candy sprinkles are all great additions to the cocktail cups.

CHAPTER 3

Infused Alcohol

You can always buy flavored alcohols for these recipes, but making your own fruit-infused alcohols is so worth the effort. The flavors are much fresher and more natural. These are very easy to make and only require 10 days of patience while the fruits soak.

You will need a large container to hold the fruit and alcohol. There are numerous decorative containers; you can use the large wide mouth canning jars or even your sun tea container! You just need to be sure the containers are air tight during the process. The decorative containers are nice to display on your counter top and will dress up your kitchen while your fruits are soaking. They will get anyone who visits intrigued and wanting to attend your next party!

I recommend making a small batch of the flavors you like in the wide mouth canning jars first. This way you can taste test various recipes and if you find a favorite you can then make a larger batch the next time around.

Store the infusing containers in your pantry. They can also be refrigerated during the infusing process if you desire. Be sure that if you leave the decorative container on your counter top it is not in direct sunlight.

Buying and Preparing Your Ingredients

As far as how much fruit you need to buy, it all depends on the size of container you are using and the size of the fruit. You will want to pack the fruit tightly in the jar or decanter.

A wide mouth canning jar holds 4 cups of liquid without any fruit.
The average sun tea container holds 18 cups of liquid without any fruit.

Examples:
For a 1.40 glass decanter, 9 x 16 oz containers of precut pineapple and 13 cups of Bacardi gold rum.

For a sun tea container I used 30 peeled whole red grapefruits and 11 cups of vodka. For a large wide mouth mason jar I used 20 ounces of various berries and 2 ½ cups of vodka.

Preparing the Fruit

Be sure to wash fruits and remove any stems or pits. If you buy the precut pineapple, mango or melons, they should be clean already.

Citrus Fruits
With lemons, limes and oranges you can cut some of them into slices and line the sides of the jars to look more decorative. If you do this, you can leave the skin on for the outside pieces only. Remove the skin for the rest of the citrus you are using to fill the interior of the jar. Be sure to remove as much of the pulp as possible, cutting very close to the flesh of the fruit. Leaving the pulp intact may make the alcohol taste bitter.

Berries
Leave all berries, including strawberries, whole. Be sure they are cleaned with stems removed. The strawberries will turn white when the liquid is ready. This is a natural process.

Bananas
Buy ripe, but not overripe, bananas. Peel them and put them in the jars either whole or in large slices.

Vodka & Rum
Be sure to use a medium grade rum or vodka which you would be able to drink straight. Less expensive rums and vodkas can leave a bad taste but, at the same time, you do not need to buy the premium alcohol either. You will want to fill the fruit packed container to the top with vodka or rum making sure that all of the fruit is covered.

Unveiling your recipes

You have been very patient and finally it's been 10 days and you are now ready to strain the fruits and bottle up your alcohol.

You will need a large bowl, a colander/strainer, cheese cloth or large tight knit sieve, coffee filters and large mouth mason jars with lids. Make sure you wash the mason jars and lids before using them.

Place the colander/strainer on top of the large bowl so that it is resting on the rim of the bowl and not on the bottom of the bowl. Lay the cheese cloth or sieve across the colander. Open the infused alcohol container and spoon the fruit over the cheese cloth or sieve. Let the fruit sit there for about 10-15 minutes. You can also press on the fruit to release any trapped alcohol. Next, remove the fruit and pour the remainder of the liquid from your container over the colander/sieve. Once the liquid has gone through the colander/sieve, pour the strained liquid into another bowl. Line the colander/sieve with a round coffee filter and place it over the original bowl. Now pour the liquid over the coffee filter to remove any extra sediment left from the first straining. You want your alcohol to be clear with the pulp and fruit pieces removed.

You can now store the liquid in the wide mouth canning jars. Be sure the jars are sealed tightly and write the name of the contents and the date on each lid. Store the jars in your refrigerator. This mixture can be stored in the refrigerator for 6-8 month's.

Now what can you do with the fruit! You can eat it, but remember it has been soaking in alcohol. It will be strong. You can also grind some of it up and add it to your favorite cocktail, eat it plain or even put it over ice cream. The fruit will only last about two or three days once removed from the alcohol. If not used within two or three days, be sure to throw it away.

Berry Infused Vodka
Makes 1 wide mouth canning jar - 4 cup size

Ingredients

6 oz each of raspberries, blueberries and blackberries
4 oz of small strawberries
(You can use one or all of the berries to your preference. Leave the fruit whole)
3 cups vodka (the amount might vary as it depends on the size of the berries)

Supplies

4 cup wide mouth canning jar & lid
Cheesecloth or fine mesh sieve
Large bowl
Coffee filter
Colander if using the cheesecloth

Directions

1. Rinse and drain the berries. Remove any stems.
2. Pack the berries tightly into the canning jar. You can make a row of each of the different berries to create a decorative look if you desire.
3. Pour the vodka over the fruit, filling it to the top.
4. Seal the jar tightly with the canning lids and wipe off any excess liquid from the jar.
5. Be sure to write the date and name of the contents on the jar lid.
6. Store the jar in your pantry or refrigerator. It can also be left on your counter but keep it out of direct sunlight.
7. Wait patiently for 10 days.
8. Remove the fruit and strain as described on page 12.
9. Store the canning jars in the refrigerator for up to 8 month's.
10. The berries are good for 2-3 days once removed from their vodka bath and are excellent over ice cream or sorbet.

Lemon Infused Vodka
Makes 1 wide mouth canning jar - 4 cup size

Ingredients
(Amount will vary with the size of the lemons)
7-10 lemons
2-3 cups vodka

Supplies
4 cup wide mouth canning jar & lid
Cheesecloth or fine mesh sieve
Large bowl
Coffee filter
Colander if using the cheesecloth

Directions
1. Peel the lemons and remove all of the skin and pulp. Leave the lemons whole. You can add a few extra lemon slices, with the skin left on, to line the sides of the jar if you wish to make it more decorative.
2. Pack the canning jar tightly with the whole lemons.
3. Pour the vodka over the fruit, filling it to the top.
4. Seal the jar tightly with the canning lids and wipe off any excess liquid from the jar.
5. Be sure to write the date and name of the contents on the jar lid.
6. Store the jar in your pantry or refrigerator. It can also be left on your counter but keep it out of direct sunlight.
7. Wait patiently for 10 days.
8. Remove the fruit and strain as described on page 12.
9. Store the canning jars in the refrigerator for up to 8 month's.

Variation to fill a sun tea container: (Amount will vary with the size of the lemons)
25-30 lemons and 12-13 cups of vodka

Lime Infused Vodka
Makes 1 wide mouth canning jar - 4 cup size

Ingredients
(Amount will vary with the size of the limes)
12-15 limes
2-3 cups vodka

Supplies
4 cup wide mouth canning jar & lid
Cheesecloth or fine mesh sieve
Large bowl
Coffee filter
Colander if using the cheesecloth

Directions
1. Peel the limes and remove all of the skin and pulp. You can add a few extra lime slices, with the skin left on, to line the sides of the jar if you wish to make it more decorative.
2. Pack the canning jar tightly with the whole limes.
3. Pour the vodka over the fruit, filling it to the top.
4. Seal the jar tightly with the canning lids and wipe off any excess liquid from the jar.
5. Be sure to write the date and name of the contents on the jar lid.
6. Store the jar in your pantry or refrigerator. It can also be left on your counter but keep it out of direct sunlight.
7. Wait patiently for 10 days.
8. Remove the fruit and strain as described on page 12.
9. Store the canning jars in the refrigerator for up to 8 month's.

Variation to fill a sun tea container: (Amount will vary with the size of the limes)
35-40 limes and 13-14 cups of vodka.)

Mango Infused Vodka
Makes 1 wide mouth canning jar - 4 cup size

Ingredients
(Amount will vary with the size of the mango slices)
16-20 ounces of mango slices
1 ½ - 2 cups vodka

Supplies
4 cup wide mouth canning jar & lid
Cheesecloth or fine mesh sieve
Large bowl
Coffee filter
Colander if using the cheesecloth

Directions
1. Peel and slice the mangos and remove the seed. You can also purchase the pre-cut slices.
2. Pack the canning jar tightly with the mangos.
3. Pour the vodka over the fruit, filling it to the top.
4. Seal the jar tightly with the canning lids and wipe off any excess liquid from the jar.
5. Be sure to write the date and name of the contents on the jar lid.
6. Store the jar in your pantry or refrigerator. It can also be left on your counter but keep it out of direct sunlight.
7. Wait patiently for 10 days.
8. Remove the fruit and strain as described on page 12.
9. Store the canning jars in the refrigerator for up to 8 month's.
10. The mangos are good for 2-3 days once removed from their vodka bath and are excellent over vanilla or coconut ice cream.

Orange Infused Vodka
Makes 1 wide mouth canning jar - 4 cup size

Ingredients
(Amount will vary with the size of the oranges)
4-6 oranges (Mandarin oranges can be substituted)
1 ½ - 2 ½ cups vodka

Supplies
4 cup wide mouth canning jar & lid
Cheesecloth or fine mesh sieve
Large bowl
Coffee filter
Colander if using the cheesecloth

Directions
1. Peel the oranges and remove all of the skin and pulp. You can add a few extra orange slices, with the skin left on, to line the sides of the jar if you wish to make it more decorative.
2. Pack the canning jar tightly with the whole oranges.
3. Pour the vodka over the fruit, filling it to the top.
4. Seal the jar tightly with the canning lids and wipe off any excess liquid from the jar.
5. Be sure to write the date and name of the contents on the jar lid.
6. Store the jar in your pantry or refrigerator. It can also be left on your counter but keep it out of direct sunlight.
7. Wait patiently for 10 days.
8. Remove the fruit and strain as described on page 12.
9. Store the canning jars in the refrigerator for up to 8 month's.

Variation to fill a sun tea container: (Amount will vary with the size of the oranges, 20-25 oranges and 11-12 cups of vodka.)

Pineapple Infused Vodka
Makes 1 wide mouth canning jar - 4 cup size

Ingredients
(Amount will vary with the size of the pineapple slices)
16-20 ounces of fresh pineapple
1 ½ - 2 cups vodka

Supplies
4 cup wide mouth canning jar &lid
Cheesecloth or fine mesh sieve
Large bowl
Coffee filter
Colander if using the cheesecloth

Directions
1. Peel, slice and core the pineapple. You can also purchase the precut slices.
2. Pack the canning jar tightly with the pineapple.
3. Pour the vodka over the fruit, filling it to the top.
4. Seal the jar tightly with the canning lids and wipe off any excess liquid from the jar.
5. Be sure to write the date and name of the contents on the jar lid.
6. Store the jar in your pantry or refrigerator. It can also be left on your counter but keep it out of direct sunlight.
7. Wait patiently for 10 days.
8. Remove the fruit and strain as described on page 12.
9. Store the canning jars in the refrigerator for up to 8 month's.
10. The pineapple is good for 2-3 days once removed from its vodka bath and is excellent over vanilla or coconut ice cream.

Variation to fill a sun tea container: (Amount will vary with the size of the pineapple slices) 18 cups sliced pineapple and 12-14 cups of vodka.

Ruby Red Grapefruit Vodka
Makes 1 wide mouth canning jar - 4 cup size

Ingredients
(Amount will vary with the size of the grapefruit)
3-4 ruby red grapefruit
1 ½ - 2 ½ cups vodka

Supplies
4 cup wide mouth canning jar &lid
Cheesecloth or fine mesh sieve
Large bowl
Coffee filter
Colander if using the cheesecloth

Directions
1. Peel the grapefruits and remove all of the skin and pulp. Place as many whole grapefruits as you can in the center of the jar and then place sliced grapefruits around the whole grapefruits to form an outer layer.
2. Pack the canning jar tightly with the grapefruit.
3. Pour the vodka over the fruit, filling it to the top.
4. Seal the jar tightly with the canning lids and wipe off any excess liquid from the jar.
5. Be sure to write the date and name of the contents on the jar lid.
6. Store the jar in your pantry or refrigerator. It can also be left on your counter but keep it out of direct sunlight.
7. Wait patiently for 10 days.
8. Remove the fruit and strain as described on page 12.
9. Store the canning jars in the refrigerator for up to 8 month's.
10. The grapefruit is good for 2-3 days once removed from its vodka bath and is excellent served on its own as a desert.

Variation to fill a sun tea container: (Amount will vary with the size of the grapefruit) 30 grapefruit and 11-12 cups of vodka.

Banana Rum
Makes 1 wide mouth canning jar - 4 cup size

Ingredients
(Amount will vary with the size of the bananas)

5-6 ripe bananas – whole or large slices

2-3 cups white rum

½ teaspoon cinnamon

½ teaspoon nutmeg

2 teaspoon brown sugar

Supplies
4 cup wide mouth canning jar &lid

Saucepan

Cheesecloth or fine mesh sieve

Large bowl

Coffee filter

Colander if using the cheesecloth

Directions
1. Combine all ingredients, except for the bananas, in a small saucepan. Simmer until the sugar has melted and all of the ingredients are mixed well. Do not boil. Remove from heat and let cool.
2. Pack the canning jar tightly with the bananas.
3. Pour the rum mixture over the bananas, filling it to the top.
4. Seal the jar tightly with the canning lids and wipe off any excess liquid from the jar.
5. Be sure to write the date and name of the contents on the jar lid.
6. Store the jar in your pantry or refrigerator. It can also be left on your counter but keep it out of direct sunlight.
7. Wait patiently for 10 days.
8. Remove the bananas and strain as described on page 12.

9. Store the canning jars in the refrigerator for up to 8 month's.
10. The bananas are good for 2-3 days once removed from their rum bath and are good warmed up and served over vanilla or coconut ice cream. The bananas will turn slightly black and do not look very attractive but they are very tasty.

Mango Rum
Makes 1 wide mouth canning jar - 4 cup size

Ingredients
(Amount will vary with the size of the mango slices)
16-20 ounces of mango slices
1 ½ - 2 cups Gold rum

Supplies
4 cup wide mouth canning jar & lid
Cheesecloth or fine mesh sieve
Large bowl
Coffee filter
Colander if using the cheesecloth

Directions
1. Peel and slice the mangos and remove the seed. You can also purchase the pre-cut slices.
2. Pack the canning jar tightly with the mangos.
3. Pour the rum over the fruit, filling it to the top.
4. Seal the jar tightly with the canning lids and wipe off any excess liquid from the jar.
5. Be sure to write the date and name of the contents on the jar lid.
6. Store the jar in your pantry or refrigerator. It can also be left on your counter but keep it out of direct sunlight.
7. Wait patiently for 10 days.
8. Remove the fruit and strain as described on page 12.
9. Store the canning jars in the refrigerator for up to 8 month's.
10. The mangos are good for 2-3 days once removed from their rum bath and are excellent over vanilla or coconut ice cream.

Pineapple Rum
Makes 1 wide mouth canning jar - 4 cup size

Ingredients
(Amount will vary with the size of the pineapple slices)
16-20 ounces of fresh pineapple
1 ½ - 2 cups gold rum
(You can also use spiced rum if you prefer)

Supplies
4 cup wide mouth canning jar &lid
Cheesecloth or fine mesh sieve
Large bowl
Coffee filter
Colander if using the cheesecloth

Directions
1. Peel, core and slice the pineapple. You can also purchase the precut slices.
2. Pack the canning jar tightly with the pineapple.
3. Pour the Rum over the fruit, filling it to the top.
4. Seal the jar tightly with the canning lids and wipe off any excess liquid from the jar.
5. Be sure to write the date and name of the contents on the jar lid.
6. Store the jar in your pantry or refrigerator. It can also be left on your counter but keep it out of direct sunlight.
7. Wait patiently for 10 days.
8. Remove the fruit and strain as described on page 12.
9. Store the canning jars in the refrigerator for up to 8 month's.
10. The pineapple is good for 2-3 days once removed from its rum bath and is excellent served over vanilla or coconut ice cream.

Variation to fill a sun tea container: (Amount will vary with the size of the pineapple slices) 18 cups sliced pineapple and 12-14 cups of rum.

CHAPTER 4

Champagne Concoctions

Brandon's Cinnamon Cyclone
Makes 4-6 Concoctions

Do falling leaves remind you of autumn? This desert will as well! Apple cider drinkers will enjoy the cinnamon spiced taste with the sweetness of champagne and fresh peeled apples.

Ingredients

1 ounce butterscotch schnapps
5 ounces fresh apple cider (from the produce refrigerated section) *
6 ounces FLAT champagne
4 teaspoons brown sugar
2 teaspoons fresh squeezed lemon juice
3 ounces Knox unflavored gelatin
Cinnamon and sugar for topping

*Fresh apple cider can be found seasonally during autumn time in your produce department.

Directions

1. Mix 1 package of the gelatin with 1 cup of boiling water. Mix well, add 1 ice cube and stir. Set aside to cool.
2. Stir the brown sugar, lemon juice and apple cider into a pourable measuring cup or pitcher. Mix well. Once the sugar has dissolved, add the schnapps and champagne. Mix well.
3. Stir in the gelatin. Mix well.
4. Pour the mixture into the molds or cups.
5. Freeze for 45-60 minutes and add the wood sticks if using Liqoursicle molds.
6. Freeze overnight.

Serving

1. You can either let the mold sit out for 3-4 minutes or run some tepid water over the mold while making sure that the water flow is below the rim of the mold.
2. Gently pull the sticks to remove.
3. If desert was frozen in a cup, take it out of the freezer and sprinkle with the sugar/cinnamon mixture. It is best served when removed from the freezer and allowed to thaw for 3-5 minutes. Enjoy!

Christmas Poinsettia
Makes 4 - 6 Concoctions

The beautiful red Christmas flower shares the vibrant color of this holiday dessert.
Champagne is used to create the holiday cheer

Ingredients
3 ounces FLAT champagne
3 ounces cranberry juice
3 ½ tablespoons canned jellied cranberry sauce
1 ½ tablespoons agave nectar
2 ounces Knox unflavored gelatin
2 drops red food color
Large sugar crystals - optional

Directions
1. Mix 1 package of the gelatin with 1 cup boiling water. Mix well, add 1 ice cube and stir. Set aside to cool.
2. Mix the jellied cranberry sauce, agave nectar, food color and 1 ounce of the cranberry juice in the blender on medium speed. Do not add all of the juice in the blender as it will become too foamy.
3. Stir in the champagne and remaining cranberry juice.
4. Stir in the gelatin. Mix well
5. Pour the mixture into molds or cups.
6. Freeze for 45-60 minutes and add the wood sticks if using Liqoursicle molds. If using cocktail cups, you can sprinkle the cups with the sugar crystals at this time.
7. Freeze overnight.

Serving
1. If you use a Liqoursicle mold, you can either let the mold sit out for 3-4 minutes or run some tepid water over the mold while making sure that the water flow

is below the rim of the mold. Gently pull the sticks to remove. Now you can sprinkle the sugar crystals lightly over the Liquorsicle.

2. If you freeze the dessert in a cup, it is best served if taken out of the freezer and allowed to thaw for 3-5 minutes. Enjoy!

Cupids Arrow Champagne
Makes 4-6 Concoctions

Plentiful amounts of fresh ripened strawberries and champagne make this dessert a captivating Valentines Day extravagance!

Ingredients

½ ounce strawberry liqueur (Italian Fragoli brand is a good one)

3 ½ ounces FLAT champagne

½ ounce fresh squeezed lemon juice

1 ounce water

7 ounces strawberry puree *

2 ½ tablespoons agave nectar

2 ounces Knox unflavored gelatin

Large sugar crystals

*Strawberry puree - Blend 7 ounces of frozen (thawed) or fresh sliced strawberries and 1 ounce of water.

Directions

1. Mix 1 package of the gelatin with 1 cup of boiling water. Mix well, add 1 ice cube and stir. Set aside to cool.
2. Stir the strawberry puree, strawberry liqueur, lemon juice and water in a pourable measuring cup or pitcher. Mix well. Stir in the agave nectar and flat champagne.
3. Stir in the gelatin. Mix well.
4. Pour the mixture into the molds or cups.
5. Freeze for 45-60 minutes and add the wood sticks if using Liqoursicle molds. If using cocktail cups, you can sprinkle the cups with the sugar crystals at this time.
6. Freeze overnight.

Serving

1. If you use a Liqoursicle mold, you can either let the mold sit out for 3-4 minutes or run some tepid water over the mold while making sure that the water flow is below the rim of the mold. Gently pull the sticks to remove. Sprinkle the molds with the sugar crystals.
2. If you freeze the dessert in a cup, it is best served when removed from the freezer and allowed to thaw for 3-5 minutes. Enjoy!

Paddy's Shamrock
Makes 4-6 Concoctions

Your Irish eyes will be smiling when you taste these shamrock colored champagne concoctions.

Ingredients

1 ¼ ounces Midori Melon Liqueur

4 ½ ounces FLAT champagne

2 ½ ounces orange juice

3 tablespoons agave nectar

4 drops green food coloring

2 ounces Knox unflavored gelatin

Directions

1. Mix 1 package of the gelatin with 1 cup boiling water. Mix well, add 1 ice cube and stir. Set aside to cool.
2. Stir all of the ingredients except the gelatin into a pourable measuring cup or pitcher. Mix well.
3. Stir in the gelatin.
4. Pour the mixture into the molds or cups.
5. Freeze for 45-60 minutes and add the wood sticks if using Liqoursicle molds.
6. Freeze overnight.

Serving

1. If you use a Liqoursicle mold, you can either let the mold sit out for 3-4 minutes or run some tepid water over the mold while making sure that the water flow is below the rim of the mold. Gently pull the sticks to remove.
2. If you freeze the dessert in a cup, it is best served if taken out of the freezer and allowed to thaw for 3-5 minutes. Enjoy!

Passionate Peach Champagne
Makes 4-6 Concoctions

Cheers! This New Year's Eve revitalizing peach and champagne dessert is the perfect way to ring in the New Year!

Ingredients

3 ½ ounces FLAT champagne
4 ounces peach nectar
4 ounces peach puree *
2 tablespoons agave nectar
2 ounces Knox unflavored gelatin
Large sugar crystals

* Peach puree- Blend 4 ounces of thawed frozen or fresh sliced peaches and 1 ounce water.

Directions

1. Mix 1 package of gelatin with 1 cup boiling water. Mix well, add 1 ice cube and stir. Set aside to cool.
2. Stir the peach nectar, peach puree, and agave nectar into a pourable measuring cup or pitcher. Mix well. Stir in the flat champagne.
3. Stir in the gelatin. Mix well.
4. Pour the mixture into molds or cups.
5. Freeze for 45-60 minutes and add the wood sticks if using Liqoursicle molds. If using cocktail cups, you can sprinkle the cups with the sugar crystals at this time.
6. Freeze overnight.

<u>Serving</u>

1. If you use a Liqoursicle mold, you can either let the mold sit out for 3-4 minutes or run some tepid water over the mold while making sure that the water flow is below the rim of the mold. Gently pull the sticks to remove. Sprinkle the molds with the sugar crystals.
2. If you freeze the dessert in a cup, it is best served if taken out of the freezer and allowed to thaw for 3-5 minutes. Enjoy!

Pomegranate Princess
Makes 6-8 Concoctions

You will not be counting down the seconds but counting how many of these delightful pomegranate and champagne treats you have on New Year's Eve.

Ingredients

3 ½ ounces FLAT champagne

1 ounce white rum

1 ounce water

6 ounces pomegranate juice

1 teaspoon fresh squeezed Lemon juice

2 ½ tablespoons agave nectar

2 tablespoons pomegranate seeds (optional - omit if you don't like the crunchy seeds)

2 ounces Knox unflavored gelatin

Large sugar crystals

Directions

1. Mix 1 package of the gelatin with 1 cup boiling water. Mix well, add 1 ice cube and stir. Set aside to cool.
2. Stir the water, pineapple juice, white rum, lemon juice and agave nectar into a pourable measuring cup or pitcher. Mix well. Add the flat champagne and pomegranate seeds. Mix well.
3. Stir in the gelatin. Mix well.
4. Pour the mixture into the molds or cups.
5. Freeze for 45-60 minutes and add the wood sticks if using liqoursicle molds. If using cocktail cups, you can sprinkle the cups with the sugar crystals at this time.
6. Freeze overnight.

Serving

1. If you use a Liqoursicle mold, you can either let the mold sit out for 3-4 minutes or run some tepid water over the mold while making sure that the water flow is below the rim of the mold. Gently pull the sticks to remove. Sprinkle the molds with the sugar crystals.

2. If you freeze the dessert in a cup, it is best served when removed from the freezer and allowed to thaw for 3-5 minutes. Enjoy!

THE MORNING AFTER

The Morning After
Makes 4-6 Concoctions

An orange juice and champagne mixture that will give you a bit of that "hair of the dog" for your New Year's Day brunch!

Ingredients

3 ounces FLAT champagne
4 ounces orange juice
3 ounces mandarin orange puree *
2 tablespoons agave nectar
2 ounces Knox unflavored gelatin
Large sugar crystals

* Mandarin orange puree- blend 3 ounces of canned mandarin oranges.

Directions

1. Mix 1 package of the gelatin and 1 cup boiling water. Mix well, add 1 ice cube and stir. Set aside to cool.
2. Stir the orange juice, orange puree and agave nectar into a pourable measuring cup or pitcher. Mix well. Stir in the flat champagne.
3. Stir in the gelatin. Mix well.
4. Pour the mixture into the molds or cups.
5. Freeze for 45-60 minutes and add the wood sticks if using Liqoursicle molds. If using cocktail cups, you can sprinkle the cups with the sugar crystals at this time.
6. Freeze overnight.

Serving

1. If you use a Liqoursicle mold, you can either let the mold sit out for 3-4 minutes or run some tepid water over the mold while making sure that the water flow is below the rim of the mold. Gently pull the sticks to remove. Sprinkle the molds with the sugar crystals. .

2. If you freeze the dessert in a cup it is best served if taken out of the freezer and allowed to thaw for 3-5 minutes. Enjoy!

CHAPTER 5

Cream Concoctions
These recipes work best as cocktail cups

Arousing Almond
Makes 4 - 6 Concoctions

The Italian sweet liquor Amaretto and creamy Cool Whip blend well to give this treat a creamy almond flavor that will keep you coming back for more!

Ingredients

2 ounces Amaretto

2 ounces cream de cacao

¼ teaspoon almond extract

6 ounces Carnation evaporated milk

3 tablespoons Cool Whip topping

2 teaspoons bar sugar*

3 ounces Knox unflavored gelatin

Nutmeg

* Bar sugar- this is a super fine sugar that dissolves quickly and can be found in liquor stores.

Directions- This recipe works best as a cocktail cup.

1. Make the package of gelatin with 1 cup boiling water. Mix well, add 1 ice cube and stir. Set aside to cool.
2. Combine the Cool Whip, sugar and Carnation milk in a blender and mix on low. Mix well.
3. Stir in the amaretto, cream de cacao and almond extract.
4. Stir in the gelatin. Do not blend or it will get foamy.
5. Pour the mixture into the cocktail cups.
6. Freeze overnight.

Serving

Take the cups out of the freezer and sprinkle lightly with nutmeg. It is best served if taken out of the freezer and allowed to thaw 3-5 minutes. Enjoy!

Banana Hammock
Makes 4 - 6 Concoctions

Tasting like a chocolate covered banana, this treat is overflowing with creamy banana flavor topped off with sweet drizzled chocolate.

Ingredients

2 ounces cream de cacao

1 ounce banana liqueur

1 ounce banana rum*

2 ounces Baileys Irish Cream

½ ripe banana - peeled

2 ½ ounces Carnation evaporated milk

1 teaspoon agave nectar

2 ½ ounces Knox unflavored gelatin

Chocolate syrup

* You can use store bought banana rum or make your own, see page 21 for infused banana rum.

Directions- This recipe works best as a cocktail cup.

1. Mix the package of gelatin with 1 cup boiling water. Mix well, add 1 ice cube and stir. Set aside to cool.
2. Mix the banana, agave nectar, banana liqueur, banana rum and cream de cacao in blender on low speed. Mix well.
3. Stir in the Baileys Irish Cream and Carnation evaporated milk. Do not blend.
4. Stir in the gelatin. Mix well.
5. Pour the mixture into the cocktail cups.
6. Freeze for 45-60 minutes and drizzle the cups with chocolate syrup.
7. Freeze overnight.

Serving

Remove the cups from the freezer. They are best served when taken out of the freezer and allowed to thaw for 3-5 minutes. Enjoy!

BANANA HAMMOCK

Baileys Bombshell
Makes 4-6 Concoctions

Tastes just like what dessert should taste like! Creamy & chocolaty!

Ingredients

1 ¾ ounces Baileys Irish Cream*
3 ounces Carnation evaporated milk
2 tablespoons Cool Whip topping
1 ½ tablespoons chocolate syrup
2 ounces Knox unflavored gelatin
Chocolate syrup for drizzle - optional

* You can use any of the Bailey's flavors of liqueur (regular, mint or caramel).

Directions- This recipe works best as a cocktail cup.

1. Mix the package of gelatin with 1 cup boiling water. Mix well, add 1 ice cube and stir. Set aside to cool.
2. Mix the Bailey's, Carnation evaporated milk, chocolate syrup and Cool Whip in a blender on low speed. Mix well.
3. Stir in the gelatin. Do not use the blender.
4. Pour the mixture into the cocktail cups.
5. Freeze for 45-60 minutes and drizzle the cups with chocolate syrup.
6. Freeze overnight.

Serving

Remove the cups from the freezer. They are best served when taken out of the freezer and allowed to thaw for 3-5 minutes. Enjoy!

Buttered Buns
Makes 4-6 Concoctions

An adult version of a buttery smooth butterscotch sundae!

Ingredients

2 ¼ ounces butterscotch schnapps

1 ½ ounces Baileys Irish Cream

2 ½ ounces Carnation evaporated milk

2 tablespoons butterscotch ice cream topping

2 ounces Knox unflavored gelatin

Butterscotch ice cream topping for drizzle

3 - 4 butterscotch hard candies - optional

Directions- This recipe works best as a cocktail cup.

1. Mix 1 package of the gelatin with 1 cup of boiling water. Mix well, add 1 ice cube and stir. Set aside to cool.
2. Stir the Carnation evaporated milk, butterscotch schnapps, butterscotch topping and Bailey's into a pourable measuring cup or pitcher and mix well.
3. Stir in the gelatin. Mix well.
4. Pour the mixture into the cocktail cups.
5. Freeze for 45-60 minutes and lightly drizzle the cups with butterscotch ice cream topping.
6. Freeze overnight.

Serving

1. Place the hard butterscotch candies between wax paper. Place on a cutting board and crush with a mallet or hammer.
2. Take the cups out of the freezer and sprinkle the broken pieces of candy over the desserts on top of the butterscotch topping. They are best served if taken out of the freezer and allowed to thaw for 3-5 minutes. Enjoy!

Candy Cane
Makes 4-6 Concoctions

Santa's favorite candy is crushed and added along with peppermint schnapps to create this creamy holiday yummyness.

Ingredients

2 ounces Godiva White Chocolate Liqueur

1 ounce peppermint schnapps

½ ounce white rum

6 ounces Carnation evaporated milk

½ teaspoon vanilla extract

¾ teaspoon bar sugar *

2 ounces Knox unflavored gelatin

2 teaspoons crushed candy cane or 3-4 peppermint hard candies -crushed

(Save the extra crushed candy for topping)

* Bar sugar- this is a super fine sugar that dissolves quickly and can be found in liquor stores

Directions- This recipe works best as a cocktail cup.

1. Mix 1 package of the gelatin with 1 cup boiling water. Mix well, add 1 ice cube and stir. Set aside to cool.
2. Stir the Godiva White Chocolate Liqueur, peppermint schnapps, rum, vanilla extract and sugar into a pourable measuring cup or pitcher. Mix well until the sugar is dissolved. Add the Carnation evaporated milk and mix.
3. Place the peppermint hard candies between wax paper and place on a cutting board. Crush with a mallet or hammer.
4. Stir in the 2 tsp. of crushed candy, saving the rest for the topping.
5. Stir in the gelatin. Mix well.
6. Pour the mixture into the cocktail cups.
7. Freeze overnight.

<u>Serving</u>

Take the cups out of the freezer and sprinkle the crushed pieces of candy over the desserts. Best served if taken out of the freezer and allowed to thaw for 3-5 minutes. Enjoy!

Captivating Caramel Tini
Makes 6 - 8 Concoctions

A creamy, sticky and cool dessert. You will be going to your freezer instead of your coffee shop for your favorite caramel treat.

Ingredients

2 ounces butterscotch schnapps
2 ounces vanilla vodka
2 ounces caramel ice cream topping
6 ounces Carnation evaporated milk
3 ounces vanilla instant pudding*
3 ounces Knox unflavored gelatin
Caramel ice cream topping to drizzle

* You can buy ready made pudding or make your own using the directions on the box.

Directions- This recipe works best as a cocktail cup.

1. Mix 1 package of the gelatin with 1 cup of boiling water. Mix well, add 1 ice cube and stir. Set aside to cool.
2. Mix the pudding, vanilla vodka, caramel topping, and butterscotch schnapps in a blender on low speed until the caramel topping is well blended.
3. Stir in the Carnation milk. Do not use the blender.
4. Stir in the gelatin. Mix well.
5. Pour the mixture into the cups.
6. Freeze for 45-60 minutes and lightly drizzle the cups with the caramel ice cream topping.
7. Freeze overnight.

Serving

If you freeze the dessert in a cup, it is best served when removed from the freezer and allowed to thaw for 3 - 5 minutes. Enjoy!

Coconut Cupcake
Makes 4-6 Concoctions

This is a coconut lover's dream! Coconut cream, coconut rum and toasted coconut topping all blend perfectly to make this luxurious dessert.

Ingredients

2 ounces coconut rum

¾ ounce fluffed marshmallow vodka

2 ounces Coco Lopez Coconut Cream

1 ½ ounce coconut water

1 teaspoon bar sugar*

2 ½ ounces Carnation evaporated milk

1/8 teaspoon coconut extract

2 ½ ounces Knox unflavored gelatin

2 ounces sweetened toasted flaked coconut**

* Bar sugar- this is a super fine sugar that dissolves quickly and can be found in liquor stores

**Heat the oven to 325 degrees. Spread 2 ounces of sweetened flaked coconut on foil and heat in the oven. Keep a constant eye on it as it will burn quickly. Keep turning the coconut for about 5 minutes or until all sides are toasted. Remove from oven and set aside to cool.

Directions- This recipe works best as a Cocktail Cup.

1. Mix 1 package of the gelatin with 1 cup of boiling water. Mix well, add 1 ice cube and stir. Set aside to cool.
2. Stir the coconut water and sugar into a pourable measuring cup or pitcher and mix until the sugar is dissolved. Add the coconut rum, fluffed marshmallow vodka and coconut extract. Mix well. Add the Coco Lopez Coconut Cream and Carnation evaporated milk. Stir until well blended.

3. Stir in the gelatin. Mix well.
4. Pour the mixture into the cocktail cups.
5. Freeze overnight.

<u>Serving</u>

Remove the cups from the freezer and sprinkle with the toasted coconut. They are best served when removed from the freezer and allowed to thaw for 3-5 minutes. Enjoy!

COCONUT CUPCAKE

Cream of the Cropsicle
Makes 6-8 Concoctions

Vanilla vodka and Cool Whip topping give this orange-obsessed creamy dessert its fluffy texture.

Ingredients

2 ounces vanilla vodka

3 ounces orange Jell-O*

5 ½ ounces orange Kool-Aid**

3 tablespoons Cool Whip topping

2 tsp bar sugar***

* Mix the orange Jell-O with 1 cup boiling water. Mix well. Add 2 ice cubes and set aside to cool.

** Mix the Kool-Aid with 3 cups water and ¾ cup of sugar.

*** Bar sugar- this is a super fine sugar that dissolves quickly and can be found in liquor stores

Directions

1. Stir the Cool Whip, sugar and vanilla vodka into a pourable measuring cup or pitcher and mix until the Cool Whip is smooth and free of lumps. You can use a whisk to reduce lumps.
2. Stir in the Kool-Aid and orange Jell-O.
3. Pour the mixture into molds or cups.
4. Freeze for 45-60 minutes and add the wood sticks if using Liqoursicle molds.
5. Freeze overnight. The mixture will separate into layers.

Serving

1. If you use a Liqoursicle mold, you can either let the mold sit out for 3-4 minutes or run some tepid water over the mold while making sure that the water flow is below the rim of the mold. Gently pull the sticks to remove.

2. If you freeze the dessert in a cup, it is best served if taken out of the freezer and allowed to thaw for 3-5 minutes. Enjoy!

DOLLY GIRL'S DEVILS DELIGHT

Dolly Girl's Devil's Delight
Makes 4-6 Concoctions

Love at first sight for any Reese's Peanut Butter lover! Throughout this entire treat, every bite has the perfect amount of chocolate, peanut butter and liquor ratio! No one flavor overpowers the others.

Ingredients

1 ounce cream de cacao

1 ¼ ounce Godiva Chocolate Liqueur

1 ounce Castries Peanut Cream Rum*

3 ½ ounces Carnation evaporated milk

1 ½ tablespoons creamy peanut butter

1 ½ ounce Knox unflavored gelatin

10 mini Reese's Peanut Butter Cups - keep cold in the refrigerator which makes them easier to chop.

Chocolate syrup to drizzle

* Castries Peanut Cream Rum can be found and ordered from most local liquor stores. I also found it on line at DrinkupNY.com. It is worth the effort to find and special order it!

Directions – This recipe is best as a cocktail cup.

1. Put your empty cocktail cups in the freezer for 20 minutes.
2. Chop up 7 cold miniature peanut butter cups into small pieces. Set aside.
3. Chop the remaining 3 cold peanut butter cups and set aside. These are for the topping.
4. Mix 1 package of the gelatin and 1 cup boiling water. Mix well, add 1 ice cube and stir. Set aside to cool.
5. Take the empty cups from the freezer and drizzle the sides generously with chocolate syrup. Put back in the freezer.

6. Mix the cream de cacao, Godiva Chocolate Liqueur, peanut butter and Castries Peanut Cream Rum in a blender on low. Mix until the peanut butter is well blended.

7. Add the Carnation evaporated milk and mix on low.

8. Stir in the gelatin.

9. Remove the chocolate drizzled cups from the freezer and pour the mixture into the cups.

10. Add the 7 chopped Reese's Peanut Butter cups into the cups along with the mixture.

11. Freeze for 45-60 minutes or until the tops are firm but not completely frozen. You can tell by touch. Drizzle the tops of the cups with more chocolate syrup and the remaining 3 chopped peanut butter cups.

12. Freeze overnight.

Serving

The cocktail cups are best served when removed from the freezer and allowed to thaw for 3-5 minutes. Enjoy!

Her Majesty's Sinful Colada
Makes 4-6 Concoctions

The silky cream of coconut and homemade infused pineapple rum in this recipe make it the best Pina Colada Concoction ever! Puerto Rico invented this but I perfected it!

Ingredients

3 ounces pineapple rum (see infused pineapple rum page 24)

2 ounces coconut water

3 ounces pineapple juice

4 ounces Coco Lopez Coconut Cream

4 teaspoons powdered sugar

3 ounces Knox unflavored gelatin

5 ice cubes

Maraschino cherries- optional

Directions

1. Mix 1 package of the gelatin with 1 cup boiling water. Mix well, add 1 ice cube and stir. Set aside to cool.
2. Mix the ice, Coco Lopez Coconut Cream, coconut water and powdered sugar in a blender on medium speed. Mix until the ice is blended.
3. Stir in the pineapple juice and pineapple rum. Mix well.
4. Stir in the gelatin. Mix well.
5. Pour the mixture into the molds or cups. You can add a maraschino cherry to the mold before freezing.
6. Freeze for 45-60 minutes and add the wood sticks if using Liqoursicle molds. You can also add a maraschino cherry to the top of the cup at this time.
7. Freeze overnight.

Serving

1. If you use a Liqoursicle mold, you can either let the mold sit out for 3-4 minutes or run some tepid water over the mold while making sure that the water flow is below the rim of the mold. Gently pull the sticks to remove.

2. If you freeze the dessert in a cup, it is best served when removed from the freezer and allowed to thaw for 3-5 minutes. Enjoy!

HER MAJESTY'S SINFUL COLADA

Island Hootch

Makes 4-6 Concoctions

You will love the creaminess of this premier dessert.

Ingredients

1 ounce white rum

1 ½ ounce Kahlua Liqueur

½ ounce cream de cacao

3 ounces Coco Lopez Coconut Cream

4 ounces Carnation evaporated milk

3 ounces Knox unflavored gelatin

Directions

1. Mix 1 package of the gelatin with 1 cup boiling water. Mix well, add 1 ice cube and stir. Set aside to cool.
2. Mix the Kahlua, rum, Cream de Cacao, and Coco Lopez Coconut Cream in a blender on low. Mix until smooth.
3. Stir in the Carnation milk. Do not blend.
4. Stir in the gelatin.
5. Pour the mixture into the molds or cups.
6. Freeze for 45-60 minutes and add the wood sticks if using Liqoursicle molds.
7. Freeze overnight.

Serving

1. If you use a Liqoursicle mold, you can either let the mold sit out for 3-4 minutes or run some tepid water over the mold while making sure that the water flow is below the rim of the mold. Gently pull the sticks to remove.
2. If you freeze the dessert in a cup, it is best served when removed from the freezer and allowed to thaw for 3-5 minutes. Enjoy!

Kahlua Dream
Makes 4-6 Concoctions

Enjoying this thick creamy delicious dessert alone is not a sin!
Really sit back and enjoy!!

Ingredients

1 ounce Kahlua

1 ounce Baileys Irish Cream

1 ounce vanilla vodka (or 1 ounce of white rum if you prefer)

4 tablespoons chocolate instant pudding*

5 ounces Carnation evaporated milk

Chocolate syrup – drizzle

2 ½ ounces Knox unflavored gelatin

* You can buy the ready made pudding or make your own using the directions on the box

Directions- This recipe works best as a cocktail cup.

1. Mix 1 package of the gelatin with 1 cup boiling water. Mix well, add 1 ice cube and stir. Set aside to cool.
2. Mix the Kahlua, Baileys, rum or vodka, and Carnation milk in a blender on low speed. Add the pudding and blend for a few seconds on low. Be sure the mixture is smooth.
3. Stir in the gelatin. Mix well.
4. Pour the mixture into a cocktail cup.
5. Freeze for 45-60 minutes and drizzle chocolate syrup over the tops of the cups.
6. Freeze overnight.

Serving

The cocktail cups are best served when removed from the freezer and allowed to thaw for 3-5 minutes. Enjoy!

Kinky Key Lime
Makes 4-5 Cocktail Cups
Or one 9" pie

One bite of this tart and creamy treat and you will think you are on Duvall Street in Key West Florida! Great lime flavor.

Ingredients for Cocktail Cups

2 ounces Ke Ke Key Lime Cream Liqueur*
¾ ounce fluffed marshmallow vodka
1 ½ ounces fresh squeezed lime juice
¼ teaspoon vanilla extract
2 ½ ounces Carnation evaporated milk
2 ½ tablespoons Cool Whip topping
2 drops green food coloring
1 ½ ounces Knox unflavored gelatin
Graham cracker crumbs for topping

Ingredients for 9" Pie

1 9" graham cracker pie shell
4 ounces Ke Ke Key Lime Liqueur*
1 ½ ounces fluffed marshmallow vodka
3 ounces fresh squeezed lime juice
½ teaspoon vanilla extract
5 ½ tablespoons Cool Whip topping
5 ounces Carnation evaporated milk
4 drops green food coloring
3 ounces Knox unflavored gelatin

* Ke KE Key Lime Cream Liqueur can be found in or ordered from most local liquor stores.

Directions

Cocktail cups

1. Mix 1 package of the gelatin with 1 cup boiling water. Mix well, add 1 ice cube and stir. Set aside to cool.
2. Mix the Ke Ke Key Lime Liqueur, fluffed marshmallow vodka, lime juice, vanilla extract, Cool Whip and food coloring in a blender on low speed. Mix until smooth.
3. Stir in the Carnation evaporated milk. Do not blend.
4. Stir in the gelatin. Mix well.
5. Pour the mixture into the cups.
6. Freeze about 45-60 minutes and sprinkle the top of the cups with the graham cracker crumbs.
7. Freeze overnight.

Serving

The cocktail cups are best served when removed from the freezer and allowed to thaw for 3-5 minutes. Enjoy!

9" Pie

Directions

1. Mix 1 package of the gelatin with 1 cup boiling water. Mix well, add 1-ice cube and stir. Set aside to cool.
2. Mix the Ke Ke Key Lime Liqueur, fluffed marshmallow vodka, lime juice, vanilla extract, Cool Whip and food coloring in a blender on low speed. Mix until smooth.
3. Stir in the Carnation evaporated milk. Do not blend.
4. Stir in the gelatin. Mix well.

5. Put the blender with the mixture in the freezer for 15 minutes to slightly thicken before putting the mixture in the pie shell.
6. Pour the mixture into the pie shell. Freeze for about 1 hour and sprinkle the top of the pie with the graham cracker crumbs.
7. Freeze over night.

Serving

The pie is best served when removed from the freezer and allowed to thaw for 5-8 minutes. Enjoy!

Magical Moves Malted Milkshake
Makes 4-6 Concoctions

Ice cream truck malt cup memories are brought back with this chocolate malt dessert!
A great combination of creamy and crunchy! Enjoy this Whopper of a cocktail cup!

Ingredients

¾ ounce cream de cacao

¾ ounce Godiva White Chocolate Liqueur

1 ounce Godiva Chocolate Liqueur

2 ounces Carnation evaporated milk

2 ½ tablespoons malted milk powder

2 tablespoons chocolate instant pudding*

1 ½ ounce Knox unflavored gelatin

2 tablespoons crushed Whoppers candy

4 tablespoons crushed Whoppers candy for topping-optional

* You can buy the ready made pudding or make your own using the directions on the box.

Directions- This recipe is best as a cocktail cup.

1. Mix 1 package of the gelatin with 1 cup boiling water. Mix well, add 1 ice cube and stir. Set aside to cool.
2. Mix the cream de cacao, Godiva White Liqueur, Godiva Chocolate Liqueur, malted milk Powder and Carnation milk in a blender on low speed. Mix well. Add the pudding and mix again.
3. Place the Whopper candy between wax paper on a cutting board and crush with a mallet or hammer.
4. Stir in the 2 tablespoons crushed Whopper candy. Save the rest for the topping.
5. Stir in the gelatin.

6. Freeze about 45-60 minutes and sprinkle the top of the cups with the remaining crushed Whooper candy (optional).
7. Freeze overnight.

Serving

1. The cocktail cups are best served when removed from the freezer and allowed to thaw for 3-5 minutes. Enjoy!

Marshmallow Elf
Makes 4-6 Concoctions

"YUM- A –Licious"! I took this quote from one of my taste testers! It perfectly describes this creamy marshmallow dessert!!

Ingredients

2 ounces Kahlua

1 ounce cream de cacao

1 ounce amaretto

3 tablespoons chocolate syrup

6 tablespoons Cool Whip topping

4 ounces Carnation evaporated milk

40-50 small size marshmallows - cut in half

2 ounces Knox unflavored gelatin

Directions - This recipe works best as a cocktail cup.

1. Mix 1 package of the gelatin with 1 cup boiling water. Mix well, add 1 ice cube and stir. Set aside to cool.
2. Mix the Kahlua, cream de cacao, amaretto and chocolate syrup in a blender on low speed. Mix well. Add the Cool Whip and Carnation milk. Mix until smooth.
3. Stir in the gelatin. Mix well.
4. Add the marshmallows to the cups and pour the mixture over the marshmallows.
5. Freeze overnight.

Serving

1. The Cocktail Cups are best served when removed from the freezer and allowed to thaw for 3-5 minutes. Enjoy!

Minty Fudge Madness
Makes 6-8 Concoctions

Cream de cacao and crème de menthe give this dessert a cool fresh minty taste with the texture of fudge.

Ingredients
2 ounces Kahlua
2 ounces Bailey's Irish Cream
4 teaspoons crème de menthe liqueur (1/2 tsp in each cup)
6 tablespoons chocolate syrup
6 ounces Carnation evaporated milk
4 tablespoons chocolate instant pudding*
3 ounces Knox unflavored gelatin
6-8 Andes mints

* You can buy ready made pudding or make your own using the directions on the box.

Directions - This recipe works best as a cocktail cup.
1. Mix 1 package of the gelatin with 1 cup boiling water. Mix well, add 1 ice cube and stir. Set aside to cool.
2. Mix the Kahlua, Baileys, Carnation milk and chocolate syrup in a blender on low speed. Add the pudding and mix till smooth.
3. Stir in the gelatin.
4. Pour the mixture into the cups. Pour ½ tsp. of the crème de menthe down the center of each cup. Do not mix.
5. Freeze for 45-60 minutes and add 1 unwrapped Andes mint to the top of each cup. Be sure the top is frozen enough to hold the mint.
6. Freeze overnight.

Serving
1. The cocktail cups are best served when removed from the freezer and allowed to thaw for 3-5 minutes. Enjoy!

Moaning Minty Chip
Makes 4-6 Concoctions

You will feel like royalty eating this luxurious green crème de menthe dessert.

Ingredients

2 ½ ounces crème de menthe liqueur

2 ½ ounces cream de cacao

7 ounces Carnation evaporated milk

1 teaspoon powdered sugar

5 tablespoons mini chocolate chips

6 teaspoons mini chocolate chips for topping

2 ½ ounce Knox unflavored gelatin

Directions- This recipe works best in a cocktail cup.

1. Mix 1 package of the gelatin with 1 cup boiling water. Mix well, add 1 ice cube and stir. Set aside to cool.
2. Stir in the crème de menthe liqueur, cream de cacao, Carnation evaporated milk and powdered sugar into a pourable measuring cup or pitcher. Stir until well mixed.
3. Stir in the gelatin.
4. Pour the mixture into the cocktail cups. Add approximately 1 tablespoon of the mini chocolate chips to each cup of mixture. You can always add more if you like a lot of chocolate chips.
5. Freeze for about 45-60 minutes and sprinkle the extra mini chocolate chips to the top of the cocktail cups.
6. Freeze overnight.

Serving

1. The cocktail cups are best served when removed from the freezer and allowed to thaw for 3-5 minutes. Enjoy!

Mocha Nut Freeze
Makes 6-8 Concoctions

Caramel Baileys Irish Cream and cream de cacao give this velvety smooth treat a slight mocha taste. The sticky caramel topping and nuts will have you feeling pampered with its richness.

Ingredients
2 ounce cream de cacao

2 ounce Caramel Baileys Irish Cream

4 ounces Carnation evaporated milk

4 tablespoons vanilla instant pudding*

2 tablespoons caramel ice cream topping

5 tablespoons chopped nuts- optional

2 ½ ounces Knox unflavored gelatin

* You can buy ready made pudding or make your own using the directions on the box.

Directions - This recipe works best in a cocktail cup.
1. Mix 1 package of the gelatin with 1 cup boiling water. Mix well, add 1 ice cube and stir. Set aside to cool.
2. Mix the cream de cacao, Caramel Baileys Irish Cream, Carnation evaporated milk, and caramel topping in a blender on low speed. Add the pudding and mix until smooth.
3. Stir in the gelatin. Mix well.
4. Pour the mixture into the cups.
5. Freeze for about 45-60 minutes and sprinkle the chopped nuts on the top of each cup.
6. Freeze overnight.

Serving

1. The cocktail cups are best served when removed from the freezer and allowed to thaw for 3-5 minutes. Enjoy!

Monkey Business
Makes 6-8 Concoctions

You will feel as mischievous as a bunch of monkeys while you enjoy this bountiful chocolate and banana combination! The peanut topping gives it a great finish!

Ingredients

1 ounce Godiva Chocolate Liqueur

2 ounce Coco Lopez Coconut Cream

3 ounces Kahlua

4 ounces Carnation evaporated milk

4 tablespoons chocolate syrup

1 ripe banana- peeled

3 ounces Knox unflavored gelatin

5 tablespoons chopped peanuts- topping

Directions- This recipe works best in a Cocktail Cup.

1. Mix 1 package of the gelatin with 1 cup boiling water. Mix well, add 1 ice cube and stir. Set aside to cool.
2. Mix the Godiva Chocolate Liqueur, Kahlua, Coco Lopez Coconut Cream, banana, Carnation evaporated milk and chocolate syrup in a blender on low medium speed. Mix until the banana is smooth.
3. Stir in the gelatin. Mix well.
4. Pour the mixture into the cups.
5. Freeze for about 45-60 minutes and sprinkle the top of the cups with the chopped peanuts.
6. Freeze overnight.

Serving

1. The cocktail cups are best served when removed from the freezer and allowed to thaw for 3-5 minutes. Enjoy!

Nana's Nutella
Makes 4-6 Concoctions

This fudgy chocolate hazelnut cocktail cup is so decadent you might have to go to confession as it makes you feel sinful for enjoying something so much!

Ingredients

6 ounces Carnation evaporated milk

3 ounces Nutella Hazelnut Spread

1 ¾ ounces fluffed marshmallow vodka

2 ounces Knox unflavored gelatin

Whipped topping- optional

Directions - This recipe works best in a Cocktail Cup.

1. Mix 1 package of the gelatin with 1 cup boiling water. Mix well, add 1 ice cube and stir. Set aside to cool.
2. Mix the Carnation evaporated milk, Nutella and fluffed marshmallow vodka in a blender on low speed. Mix until smooth.
3. Stir in the gelatin. Mix well.
4. Pour the mixture into the cups.
5. Freeze overnight.

Serving

1. The cocktail cups are best served when removed from the freezer and allowed to thaw for 3-5 minutes. Enjoy!
2. Top each cup with generous amounts of whipped cream and Enjoy!

Nick the Nutty Nudist
Makes 4 - 6 Concoctions

Enjoy a lasting creamy nutty flavor in this hazelnut liqueur dessert.

Ingredients

1 ¼ ounce Frangelico Hazelnut Liqueur

¾ ounce cream de cacao

¾ ounce Bailey's Irish Cream

2 ounces Carnation evaporated milk

½ teaspoon chocolate syrup

3 tablespoons chopped nuts- can be used as a topping or added to the mixture

2 ounces Knox unflavored gelatin

Directions

1. Mix 1 package of the gelatin with 1 cup boiling water. Mix well, add 1 ice cube and stir. Set aside to cool.
2. Stir the Frangelico, cream de cacao, Bailey's Irish Cream and chocolate syrup into a pourable measuring cup or pitcher and mix well. Add the Carnation evaporated milk and stir. Add the chopped nuts to the mixture or reserve and add the nuts to the top once frozen.
3. Stir in the gelatin. Mix well.
4. Pour the mixture into the molds or cups.
5. Freeze for 45-60 minutes and add the wood sticks if using Liqoursicle molds.
6. Freeze overnight.

Serving

1. If you use a Liqoursicle mold, you can either let the mold sit out for 3-4 minutes or run some tepid water over the mold while making sure that the water flow is below the rim of the mold. Gently pull the sticks to remove. You can then sprinkle nuts over the molds (optional).

2. The cocktail cups are best served when removed from the freezer and allowed to thaw for 3-5 minutes.

3. Sprinkle the top of each cup with nuts (optional). Enjoy!

Peach Whip
Makes 4-6 Cocktail Cups

Peach schnapps and fresh peaches make a scrumptious, sweet and juicy dessert! Add the creamy Cool Whip peach layer and you now have a very posh display of luxury.

<u>Ingredients for peach layer</u>

6 ounces peach puree*

2 ½ ounces peach schnapps

3 ounces peach nectar

2 tablespoons peach jam

1 tablespoon bar sugar**

1 ½ ounces Knox unflavored gelatin

Whipped cream for topping- optional

<u>Ingredients for Cream Layer</u>

1 ½ ounces peach schnapps

2 ounces Carnation evaporated milk

5 ounces Cool Whip topping

2 ounces peach nectar

1 ounce peach puree*

3 teaspoons bar sugar**

1 ounce Knox unflavored gelatin

*Peach puree-Blend 7 ounces of fresh sliced or frozen (thawed) peaches and 1 ounce of water.

** Bar sugar- this is a super fine sugar that dissolves quickly and can be found in liquor stores.

Directions- Peach Layer

1. Mix 1 package of the gelatin with 1 cup boiling water. Mix well, add 1 ice cube and stir. Set aside to cool.
2. Mix the peach puree, peach schnapps, sugar, peach jam and peach nectar in a blender on low speed.
3. Pour the mixture into a pourable measuring cup or pitcher.
4. Stir in 1 ½ ounces of the gelatin. Stir the remaining gelatin a few times while it sits so the gelatin does not set. (If it does set you can microwave it 15-20 seconds to liquefy. Do not use it in the gel form)
5. Pour 1/3 of the mixture into the cups and freeze for about 1 hour until the top is not totally frozen but not soft either.
6. Keep the remaining mixture aside for the final top of the cocktail cup. Stir a few times while it sits so the gelatin does not set.

Directions for the Cream Layer

1. Mix the peach schnapps, peach nectar, Carnation evaporated milk, peach puree, sugar and Cool Whip in a blender on low speed. Mix until smooth.
2. Stir in 1 ounce of the Knox unflavored gelatin.
3. Remove the cups from the freezer; be sure the layer is slightly frozen and not soft.
4. Pour the cream layer over the frozen layer of the cups.
5. Freeze for about 45- 60 minutes.
6. Pour the remaining peach mixture on top of the cream layer.
7. Freeze overnight.

Serving

1. The cocktail cups are best served when removed from the freezer and allowed to thaw for 3-5 minutes.
2. Top each cup with generous amounts of whipped Cream. Enjoy!

Pleasing Pistachio Cloud
Makes 6-8 Concotions

A fluffy cream of marshmallows and pistachio pudding for sweetness and pineapple rum for that something something!

Ingredients

1 ½ ounces pineapple rum (see infused pineapple rum page 24)

3 ounces dry Jell-O Pistachio pudding mix

4 ounces milk

3 ounces Cool Whip topping

3 tablespoons crushed canned pineapple- do not drain

4 ounces marshmallows- small size (1/2 cup)

1 ½ ounces Knox unflavored gelatin

Directions- This recipe works best in a cocktail cup or one large bowl.

1. Mix 1 package of the gelatin with 1 cup boiling water. Mix well, add 1 ice cube and stir. Set aside to cool.
2. Mix the pudding mix and milk in a bowl. Mix well.
3. Add the Cool Whip and pineapple rum. Mix until smooth.
4. Stir in the crushed pineapple. Mix well.
5. Stir in the marshmallows.
6. Stir in the gelatin.
7. Pour the mixture into cups. You can also put this mixture in one large bowl, freeze it and scoop it out like ice cream when serving.
8. Freeze overnight.

Serving

1. The cocktail cups are best served when removed from the freezer and allowed to thaw for 3-5 minutes. Enjoy!

Precarious Pumpkin
Makes 4-6 Cocktail Cups

This dessert will be replacing the traditional pumpkin pie at your Thanksgiving table! Pumpkin liqueur & pumpkin vodka will make those family holidays a lot more tolerable!

Ingredients
1 ounce pumpkin vodka*
3 ounces pumpkin cream liqueur*
¾ ounce Bailey's Irish Cream
2 ½ teaspoons bar sugar**
5 tablespoons Libby's canned pumpkin puree
6 ice cubes
1/8 teaspoon ground cinnamon
1/8 teaspoon ground mace
1/8 teaspoon ground ginger
2 ounces Knox unflavored gelatin
Whipped cream- topping

* Pumpkin vodka and pumpkin cream liqueur can be found seasonally during Thanksgiving time at your local liquor stores.

** Bar sugar- this is a super fine sugar that dissolves quickly and can be found in liquor stores.

Directions
1. Mix 1 package of the gelatin with 1 cup boiling water. Mix well, add 1 ice cube and stir. Set aside to cool.
2. Mix the pumpkin vodka, pumpkin puree, sugar, cinnamon, ground mace, ground ginger and ice in a blender on medium speed. Mix until the ice is blended.

3. Stir in the Bailey's Irish Cream and pumpkin cream liqueur. Do not blend in the blender or it will foam.
4. Stir in the gelatin.
5. Pour the mixture into the cups.
6. Freeze overnight.

<u>Serving</u>

1. The cocktail cups are best served when removed from the freezer and allowed to thaw for 3-5 minutes.
2. Top with generous amounts of whipped topping on each cup. Enjoy!

QUEEN B'S COCONUT QUEST

Queen B's Coconut Quest
Makes 4-6 Concoctions

Two of my favorite foods: coconut and chocolate all in one creamy dish.

Ingredients

2 ounces coconut rum

2 ounces Godiva Chocolate Liqueur

½ ounce triple sec

2 ounces chocolate syrup

4 ounces Carnation evaporated milk

1 Plain 1.1 ounce chocolate bar shaved - for topping

4 tablespoons shaved sweetened coconut - for topping

3 ounces Knox unflavored gelatin

Directions - This recipe works best as a Cocktail Cup.

1. Mix 1 package of the gelatin with 1 cup boiling water. Mix well, add 1 ice cube and stir. Set aside to cool.
2. Stir the coconut rum, Godiva Chocolate Liqueur, trip sec, and chocolate syrup into a pourable measuring cup or pitcher. Mix well. Add the Carnation evaporated milk and stir until all ingredients are mixed.
3. Stir in the gelatin. Mix well.
4. Pour the mixture into the cups.
5. Freeze for about 45-60 minutes and sprinkle the top of the cups with the shaved chocolate bar.
6. Freeze overnight.

Serving

1. The cocktail cups are best served when removed from the freezer and allowed to thaw for 3-5 minutes.
2. When ready to serve, add the shredded coconut to the top of the cups. Enjoy!

Randy Russian
Makes 4-6 Concoctions

The sweetness from the marshmallow vodka gives this dessert an extra smooth creamy taste similar to a White Russian.

Ingredients

1 ½ ounces fluffed marshmallow vodka

2 ounces Kahlua

6 ounces Carnation evaporated milk

3 teaspoons bar sugar*

2 ½ ounces Knox unflavored gelatin

*Bar sugar- this is a super fine sugar that dissolves quickly and can be found in liquor stores.

Directions

1. Mix 1 package of the gelatin with 1 cup boiling water. Mix well, add 1 ice cube and stir. Set aside to cool.
2. Stir the fluffed marshmallow vodka, Kahlua, Carnation evaporated milk and bar sugar into a pourable measuring cup or pitcher. Mix well.
3. Stir in the gelatin. Mix well.
4. Pour the mixture into the molds or cups.
5. Freeze for 45-60 minutes and add the wood sticks if using Liqoursicle molds.
6. Freeze overnight.

Serving

1. If you use a Liqoursicle mold, you can either let the mold sit out for 3-4 minutes or run some tepid water over the mold while making sure that the water flow is below the rim of the mold. Gently pull the sticks to remove.
2. If you freeze the dessert in a cup, it is best served when removed from the freezer and allowed to thaw for 3-5 minutes. Enjoy!

Sassy Sassafras
Makes 6-8 Concoctions

This frosty and creamy root beer cocktail cup brings back fond memories of my grandma making me a Black Cow float for a special treat.

Ingredients

1 ounce Bailey's Irish Cream
2 ½ ounces root beer schnapps
4 ½ ounces FLAT root beer soda
1 ounce Carnation evaporated milk
3 ounces Cool Whip topping
1 teaspoon bar sugar*
Whipped cream - for topping optional
2 ounces Knox unflavored gelatin

* Bar sugar- this is a super fine sugar that dissolves quickly and can be found in liquor stores.

Directions- This recipe works best as a Cocktail Cup.

1. Mix 1 package of the gelatin with 1 cup boiling water. Mix well, add 1 ice cube and stir. Set aside to cool.
2. Stir the Cool Whip, Carnation milk, and bar sugar into a pourable measuring cup or pitcher. Stir until smooth. If there are lumps from the Cool Whip, you can use a wire whisk to reduce them.
3. Stir in the Bailey's Irish Cream, root beer schnapps, and FLAT root beer soda.
4. Stir in the gelatin. Mix well.
5. Pour the mixture into the cups.
6. Freeze overnight.

Serving

1. The cocktail cups are best served when removed from the freezer and allowed to thaw for 3-5 minutes.
2. Top each cup with a generous portion of whipped cream. Enjoy!

Skinny Dipper
Makes 4-6 Concoctions

This concoction is a beautiful turquoise color like the waters of Cancun, Mexico! It has a hearty pineapple and creamy taste with a kick that will make you wonder what happened to your bikini top!

Ingredients

2 ounces pineapple rum (see infused pineapple rum page 24)

1 ounce blue curacao

2 ounces Coco Lopez Coconut Cream

4 ounces pineapple juice

4 teaspoons agave nectar

4 ice cubes

2 ½ ounces Knox unflavored gelatin

Directions

1. Mix 1 package of the gelatin with 1 cup boiling water. Mix well, add 1 ice cube and stir. Set aside to cool.
2. Add the ice cubes, agave nectar, blue curacao and Coco Lopez Coconut Cream into a blender. Mix until the ice is blended.
3. Stir in the pineapple juice and pineapple rum. Do not blend as it will foam.
4. Stir in the gelatin. Mix well.
5. Pour the mixture in the molds or cups.
6. Freeze for 45-60 minutes and add the wood sticks if using Liqoursicle molds.
7. Freeze overnight.

Serving

1. If you use a Liqoursicle mold, you can either let the mold sit out for 3-4 minutes or run some tepid water over the mold while making sure that the water flow is below the rim of the mold. Gently pull the sticks to remove.
2. If you freeze the dessert in a cup, it is best served when removed from the freezer and allowed to thaw for 3-5 minutes. Enjoy!

Sticky Caramel Apple
Makes 4-6 Concoctions

This is a caramel apple in a cocktail cup! A gooey, buttery and nutty apple flavor is the perfect Halloween treat to share.

Ingredients

3 ounces Bailey's Caramel Liqueur

1 ½ ounces apple vodka

4 ounces fresh apple cider (from the produce department)

8 ounces natural applesauce

2 tablespoons caramel ice cream topping

2 ½ ounce Knox unflavored gelatin

Caramel ice cream topping - for topping

Chopped peanuts - for topping

Directions - This recipe works best as a cocktail cup.

1. Mix 1 package of the gelatin with 1 cup boiling water. Mix well, add 1 ice cube and stir. Set aside to cool.
2. Mix the Bailey's Caramel Liqueur, apple vodka, applesauce, apple cider and caramel topping in a blender on low speed. Mix well.
3. Stir in the gelatin. Mix well.
4. Pour the mixture into cocktail cups.
5. Freeze for about 45-60 minutes and drizzle the extra caramel topping over the cups. Sprinkle the chopped peanuts over the caramel topping.
6. Freeze overnight.

Serving

1. The cocktail cups are best served when removed from the freezer and allowed to thaw for 3-5 minutes. Enjoy

Tradewinds
Makes 4-6 Concoctions

Enjoying this tropical pineapple dessert while relaxing in the warm breezes of summer is the perfect plan for the day.

Ingredients

1 ½ ounces banana liqueur
2 ounces Midori Melon Liqueur
4 ounces pineapple juice
4 ounces orange juice
1 ounce Coco Lopez Coconut Cream
5 ice cubes
2 ½ ounces Knox unflavored gelatin
Maraschino cherries - optional

Directions

1. Mix 1 package of the gelatin with 1 cup boiling water. Mix well, add 1 ice cube and stir. Set aside to cool.
2. Mix the ice, Coco Lopez Coconut Cream, banana liqueur and Midori Melon Liqueur in a blender on medium speed.
3. Stir in the orange juice and pineapple juice.
4. Stir in the gelatin. Mix well.
5. Pour the mixture into the molds or cups. If you would like to add some maraschino cherries to the molds, cut them in half. Pour a small amount of the mixture in the molds and freezer for 20 minutes. Take out of the freezer, add the cut cherries and add the remaining mixture and freeze overnight.
6. If you are making them in cocktail cups, pour the mixture into the cups and freeze. After about 45-60 minutes, add a whole cherry to the top of each cup.
7. Freeze for 45-60 minutes and add the wood sticks if using Liqoursicle molds.
8. Freeze overnight.

Serving

1. If you use a Liqoursicle mold, you can either let the mold sit out for 3-4 minutes or run some tepid water over the mold while making sure that the water flow is below the rim of the mold. Gently pull the sticks to remove.
2. The Cocktail Cups are best served when removed from the freezer and allowed to thaw for 3-5 minutes.

WHITE CHOCOLATE BUNNY

White Chocolate Bunny
Makes 4-6 Cocktail Cups

Marshmallow vodka and Godiva White Chocolate Liqueur make this irresistible blend of enticing cream.

Ingredients

1 ounce fluffed marshmallow vodka or vanilla vodka

3 ounces Godiva White Chocolate Liqueur

7 ounces Carnation evaporated milk

8 tablespoons Cool Whip topping

1 teaspoon vanilla extract

4 teaspoons bar sugar*

3 ½ ounces Knox unflavored gelatin

3.5 oz Godiva, Lindt or Ghiradelli White Chocolate candy bar- melted

3.5 -oz Godiva, Lindt or Ghairadelli White Chocolate candy bar- grated

* Bar sugar- this is a super fine sugar that dissolves quickly and can be found in liquor stores.

Directions – This recipe works best as a cocktail cup.

1. Mix 1 package of the gelatin with 1 cup boiling water. Mix well, add 1 ice cube and stir. Set aside to cool.
2. Melt 4 squares of the Godiva chocolate bar.
3. Add the fluffed marshmallow vodka, Godiva White Chocolate Liqueur, melted chocolate bar, bar sugar and vanilla extract into the blender and mix on low speed. Mix well. Add the Cool Whip and mix until smooth.
4. Stir in the gelatin. Mix well.
5. Pour the mixture into the cups. Freeze for about 45-60 minutes. Top the cups with grated Godiva White Chocolate bar.
6. Freeze overnight.

<u>Serving</u>

1. The cocktail cups are best served when removed from the freezer and allowed to thaw for 3-5 minutes. Enjoy!

WICKED WITCHES BREW

Wicked Witches Brew
Makes 4-6 Concoctions

Don't let the funky green color keep you away from enjoying these tasty creamy Halloween treats! They are a perfect addition to your Halloween party.

Ingredients

2 ounces Kahlua

1 ½ ounces Midori Melon Liqueur

2 ounces banana liqueur

1 ripe banana

3 ½ ounces Carnation evaporated milk

3 ounces pineapple juice

5 drops green food color

3 ounces Knox unflavored gelatin

Candy corn - optional

Directions- This recipe works best as a Cocktail Cup.

1. Mix 1 package of the gelatin with 1 cup boiling water. Mix well, add 1 ice cube and stir. Set aside to cool.
2. Add the Kahlua, Midori, banana liqueur, ripe banana and food color into a blender and mix on low.
3. Stir in the Carnation evaporated milk and pineapple juice. Do not blend as mixture will foam.
4. Stir in the gelatin. Mix well.
5. Pour the mixture into the cups.
6. Freeze overnight.

Serving

1. The cocktail cups are best served when removed from the freezer and allowed to thaw for 3-5 minutes.
2. You can add a piece of candy corn to the top of each cup (optional). Enjoy!

CHAPTER 6

Fruit Concoctions

These recipes work best as Liqoursicle molds
but can also be made into cocktail cups

Aaliyah's Amazing
Makes 6-8 Concoctions

Enjoy a harmonious mixture of peach schnapps and fruit juices in this pleasing concoction.

Ingredients

2 ounces vodka

2 ounces peach schnapps

5 ounces cranberry juice

4 ounces orange juice

3 tablespoons agave nectar

1 teaspoon grenadine

3 ounces Knox unflavored gelatin

Large sugar crystals – optional

Directions

1. Mix 1 package of the gelatin with 1 cup boiling water. Mix well, add 1 ice cube and stir. Set aside to cool.
2. Stir the vodka, peach schnapps, cranberry juice, orange juice, agave nectar and grenadine into a pourable measuring cup or pitcher.
3. Stir in the gelatin. Mix well.
4. Pour the mixture into the molds or cups.
5. If you are using a Liqoursicle mold, freeze for 45-50 minutes and add the wood sticks. If you freeze the recipe in cups, you can now sprinkle them with the sugar crystals.
6. Freeze overnight.

Serving

1. If you use a Liqoursicle mold, you can either let the mold sit out for 3-4 minutes or run some tepid water over the mold while making sure that the water flow

is below the rim of the mold. Gently pull the sticks to remove. Now you can sprinkle the sugar crystals over the Liqoursicles.

2. If you freeze the dessert in a cup, it is best served when removed from the freezer and allowed to thaw for 3-5 minutes. Enjoy!

ALANA'S ALMOND

Alana's Almond
Makes 6-8 Concoctions

Amaretto makes this sweet and sour treat full bodied!

Ingredients

4 ½ ounces amaretto

6 ounces orange juice

4 ounces sweet & sour

3 tablespoons agave nectar

3 ½ ounces Knox unflavored gelatin

Maraschino cherries- optional

Large sugar crystals-optional

Directions

1. Mix 1 package of the gelatin with 1 cup boiling water. Mix well, add 1 ice cube and stir. Set aside to cool.
2. Stir the amaretto, orange juice, sweet & sour and agave nectar into a pourable measuring cup or pitcher. Mix well.
3. Stir in the gelatin.
4. Pour the mixture into the molds or cups. If you want to add some maraschino cherries to the molds, put about 1/3 of the liquid into the molds and freeze for 20 minutes, take them out of the freezer, add the chopped or whole cherries and add more liquid in the mold to cover the cherries. Freeze for 20 minutes and then add the remainder of the liquid to the molds. If you used a cup, you can add the cherries right away to the liquid and freeze it. You can also take the cups from the freezer after 1 hour and add a whole or chopped cherry and sugar crystals to the top of the cups and return them to the freezer.
5. If you are using a Liqoursicle mold, freeze for 45-50 minutes and add the wood sticks.
6. Freeze overnight.

Serving

1. If you use a Liqoursicle mold, you can either let the mold sit out for 3-4 minutes or run some tepid water over the mold while making sure that the water flow is below the rim of the mold. Gently pull the sticks to remove. You can then sprinkle the sugar crystals lightly over the Liqoursicles.

2. If you freeze the dessert in a cup, it is best served when removed from the freezer and allowed to thaw for 3-5 minutes. Enjoy!

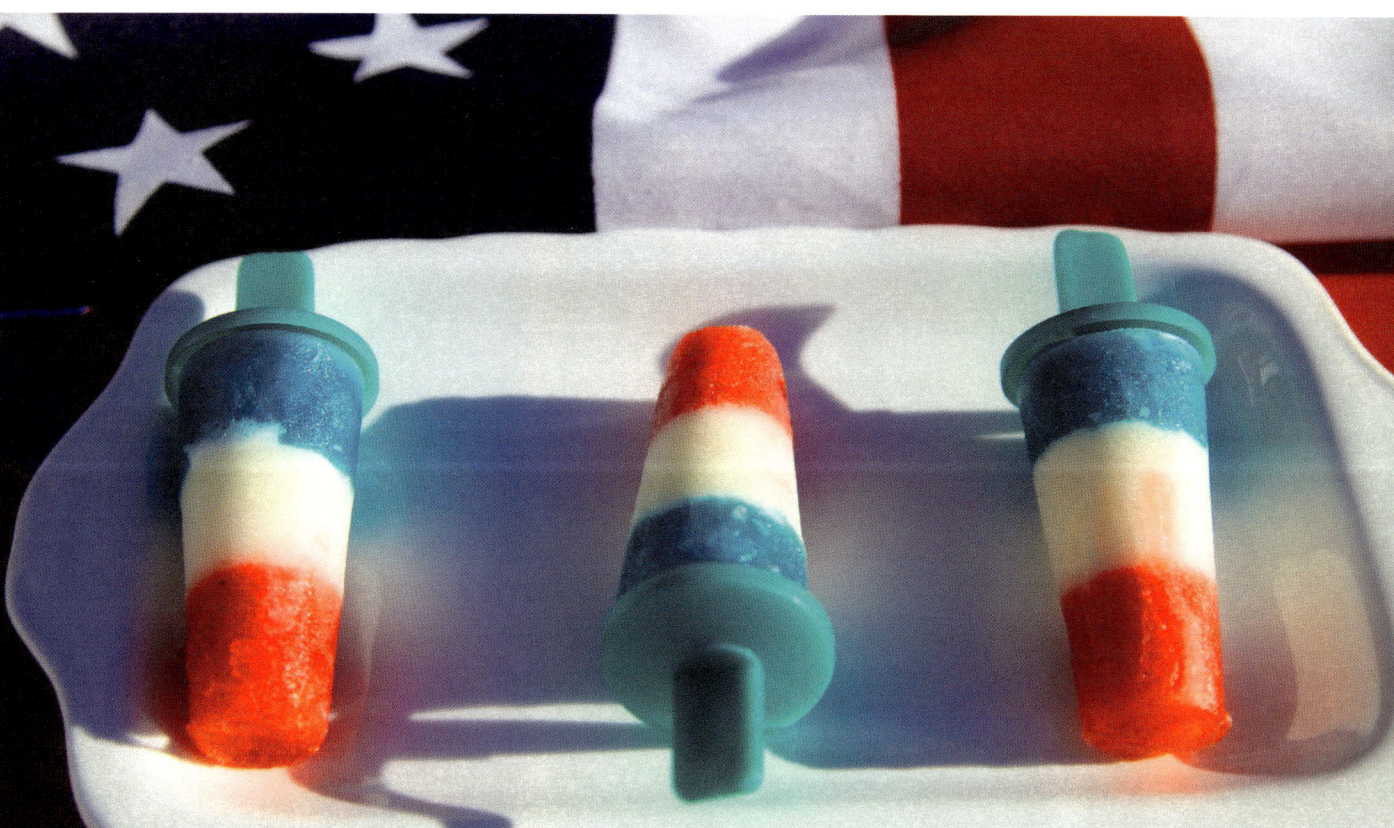

AMERICAN FLAG

American Flag
Makes 6-8 Concoctions

When you see the American flag, it brings great pride and passion for our country. These fruit flavored treats are great displays for any patriotic holiday.

Ingredients

This recipe is a red, white, and blue layered dessert made from three Rum recipes.

RED

1 ounce rum

1 ounce Fagoli Strawberry Liqueur or other brands

5 ounces strawberry puree

¾ ounce fresh squeezed Lime juice

3 ice cubes

1 tablespoon agave nectar

1 drop red food coloring

2 ounces Knox unflavored gelatin

WHITE

1 ½ ounces pineapple rum (see infused pineapple rum page 24)

1 ounce coconut water

1 ½ ounces pineapple juice

2 ounces Coco Lopez Coconut Cream

2 teaspoons powdered sugar

2 ounces Knox unflavored gelatin

3 ice cubes

BLUE

1 ounce pineapple rum (see infused pineapple rum page 24)

1 ounce blue curacao

3 ounces pineapple juice

2 drops blue food coloring

1 tablespoon agave nectar

2 ounces Knox unflavored gelatin

Directions

1. Mix 1 package of the gelatin with 1 cup boiling water. Mix well, add 1 ice cube and stir. Set aside to cool.

2. **Red Layer**- Add all of the ingredients except the gelatin into a blender and mix on medium speed. Mix until the ice is blended. Stir in the gelatin. Pour this mixture through a funnel into the molds or cups. (By using a funnel the sides of the mold or cup will not get splashed with the mixture. Freeze for 45-60 minutes.

3. **White Layer**- Add all the ice, Coco Lopez Coconut Cream, powdered sugar and coconut water into a blender and mix on medium speed. Stir in the pineapple juice and pineapple rum. Do not blend as mixture will foam. Stir in the gelatin.

4. Remove the molds or cups from the freezer. Make sure the top of the first layer is almost frozen. If you used a mold, put the wood sticks into the red layer of the mold at this time. You can now pour the white mixture through the funnel into the molds or cups. Freeze again for 45-60 minutes.

5. **Blue Layer**- Stir all of the ingredients except the gelatin into a pourable measuring cup or pitcher. Mix well. Add the gelatin and stir. You can now pour the blue layer through a funnel on top of the white layer. Be sure the white layer is frozen enough that the blue layer will not penetrate it. You can tell by touching it lightly.

6. Freeze overnight.

Note: If your container of gelatin starts to thicken while waiting for each layer to freeze, you can put the gelatin container in the microwave for 10-15 seconds to melt it. It must be in liquid form to use.

<u>Serving</u>

1. If you use a Liqoursicle mold, you can either let the mold sit out for 3-4 minutes or run some tepid water over the mold while making sure that the water flow is below the rim of the mold. Gently pull the sticks to remove.
2. If you freeze the dessert in a cup, it is best served when removed from the freezer and allowed to thaw for 3-5 minutes. Enjoy!

Andy's Twisted Trucker
Makes 4-6 Concoctions

An ongoing orange flavor that will have you thinking of a just-picked orange that was freshly squeezed.

Ingredients

1 ½ ounces orange vodka (see infused orange vodka page 18)

½ ounce Cointreau Liqueur

3 ½ ounces orange juice

2 ½ ounces cranberry juice

2 tablespoons agave nectar

1 drops red food coloring

2 drops yellow food coloring

2 ounces Knox unflavored gelatin

Directions

1. Mix 1 package of the gelatin with 1 cup boiling water. Mix well, add 1 ice cube and stir. Set aside to cool.
2. Stir all of the ingredients except the gelatin into a pourable measuring cup or pitcher. Mix well.
3. Stir in the gelatin.
4. Pour the mixture into the molds or cups.
5. Freeze for 45-60 minutes and add the wood sticks if using a Liqoursicle mold.
6. Freeze overnight.

Serving

1. If you use a Liqoursicle mold, you can either let the mold sit out for 3-4 minutes or run some tepid water over the mold while making sure that the water flow is below the rim of the mold. Gently pull the sticks to remove.

2. If you freeze the dessert in a cup, it is best served when removed from the freezer and allowed to thaw for 3-5 minutes. Enjoy!

Angela's Apricot
Makes 4-6 Concoctions

This bright orange dessert gets it smooth fragrant taste from the apricot brandy and sweetness from the apricot pie filling!

Ingredients

½ ounce white rum

1 ounce apricot brandy

2 ¾ ounces orange juice

½ ounce fresh squeezed lemon juice

4 ounces apricot pie filling

4 ice cubes

1 tablespoon agave nectar

2 ounces Knox unflavored gelatin

Directions

1. Mix 1 package of the gelatin with 1 cup boiling water. Mix well, add 1 ice cube and stir. Set aside to cool.
2. Combine the ice cubes, white rum, apricot brandy, apricot pie filling and agave nectar in a blender and mix on medium until well blended. Stir in the orange juice and lemon juice.
3. Stir in the gelatin.
4. Pour the mixture into the molds or cups.
5. Freeze for 45-60 minutes and add the wood sticks if using Liqoursicle molds.
6. Freeze overnight.

Serving

1. If you use a Liqoursicle mold, you can either let the mold sit out for 3-4 minutes or run some tepid water over the mold while making sure that the water flow is below the rim of the mold. Gently pull the sticks to remove.

2. If you freeze the dessert in a cup, it is best served when removed from the freezer and allowed to thaw for 3-5 minutes. Enjoy!

ANGIE'S APRICOT/LORI'S LUSCIOUS LEMON

Lori's Luscious Lemon
Makes 6-8 Concoctions

Cao Bella! This Italian lemon liqueur with fresh squeezed lemons will have you surprised at its smooth flavor.

Ingredients

2 ounces lemon vodka (see infused lemon vodka page 15)

4 ounces limoncello lemon liqueur

10 ounces boiling water

5 ½ ounces bar sugar*

2 tablespoons fresh lemon peel

8 ounces fresh squeezed lemon juice

1 drop yellow food coloring

3 ounces Knox unflavored gelatin

Large sugar crystals

* Bar sugar- this is a super fine sugar that dissolves quickly and can be found in liquor stores.

Directions

1. Stir the sugar into the boiling water. Stir until the sugar dissolves. Add the lemon rind. Let cool.
2. Mix 1 package of the gelatin with 1 cup boiling water. Mix well, add 1 ice cube and stir. Set aside to cool.
3. Strain the mixture through a sieve into a bowl and remove the rind.
4. Stir in the fresh squeezed lemon juice, limoncello liqueur, lemon vodka and food coloring.
5. Stir in the gelatin.
6. Pour the mixture into the molds or cups.
7. Freeze for 45-60 minutes and add the wood sticks if using Liqoursicle molds.
8. Freeze overnight.

<u>Serving</u>

1. If you use a Liqoursicle mold, you can either let the mold sit out for 3-4 minutes or run some tepid water over the mold while making sure that the water flow is below the rim of the mold. Gently pull the sticks to remove. Sprinkle with the large sugar crystals.
2. If you freeze the dessert in a cup, it is best served when removed from the freezer and allowed to thaw for 3-5 minutes. Sprinkle each cup with the large sugar crystals. Enjoy!

Berry Pucker
Makes 6-8 Concoctions

A flavorful frozen mixture of pureed fruit that will make you wonder where the alcohol is!

Ingredients

1 ounce dark rum

3/4 ounce light rum

2 ounces pineapple juice

1 ounce orange juice

3 ounces raspberry puree*

3 ounces pineapple puree**

2 tablespoons agave nectar

2 ounces Knox unflavored gelatin

Large sugar crystals

* Raspberry puree- Blend 3 ounces of frozen (thawed) or fresh raspberries and 1 ounce water.

** Pineapple puree- Blend 3 ounces of frozen (thawed) or fresh pineapple and 1 ounce water.

Directions

1. Mix 1 package of the gelatin with 1 cup boiling water. Mix well, add 1 ice cube and stir. Set aside to cool.
2. Combine the dark rum, light rum, raspberry puree, pineapple puree and agave nectar in a blender and mix on low speed. Mix well.
3. Stir in the pineapple juice and orange juice.
4. Stir in the gelatin. Mix well.
5. Pour the mixture in the molds or cups.

6. Freeze for 45 -60 minutes and add the wood sticks if using Liqoursicle molds.

7. Freeze overnight.

Serving

1. If you use a Liqoursicle mold, you can either let the mold sit out for 3-4 minutes or run some tepid water over the mold while making sure that the water flow is below the rim of the mold. Gently pull the sticks to remove. Sprinkle the molds with the large sugar crystals.

2. If you freeze the dessert in a cup, it is best served when removed from the freezer and allowed to thaw for 3-5 minutes. Sprinkle with the large sugar crystals. Enjoy!

Blast Off Banana
Makes 4-6 Concoctions

This blue curacao and banana Concoction tastes as mesmerizing as the view of the aqua waters in the Caribbean.

Ingredients

1 ounce blue curacao

2 ounces banana liqueur

1 ripe banana

2 ounces cranberry juice

1 ½ tablespoons agave nectar

3 ice cubes

2 ounces Knox unflavored gelatin

Directions

1. Mix 1 package of the gelatin with 1 cup boiling water. Mix well, add 1 ice cube and stir. Set aside to cool.
2. Combine the ice, ripe banana, blue curacao, banana liqueur and agave nectar in a blender. Mix on medium speed until the ice is blended.
3. Stir in the cranberry juice.
4. Stir in the gelatin. Mix well.
5. Pour the mixture into the molds or cups.
6. Freeze for 45-60 minutes and add the wood sticks if using Liqoursicle molds.
7. Freeze overnight.

Serving

1. If you use a Liqoursicle mold, you can either let the mold sit out for 3-4 minutes or run some tepid water over the mold while making sure that the water flow is below the rim of the mold. Gently pull the sticks to remove.
2. If you freeze the dessert in a cup, it is best served when removed from the freezer and allowed to thaw for 3-5 minutes. Enjoy!

Blushing Baked Apple
Makes 4-6 Concoctions

Spiced rum and cinnamon make this delicious apple dessert great for a fall celebration.

Ingredients

1 ounce spiced rum

¼ ounce triple sec

1 ½ ounce sweet & sour

4 ounces natural applesauce

1 teaspoon agave nectar

2 ice cubes

2 ounces Knox unflavored gelatin

1 shake cinnamon + extra for topping

Directions

1. Mix 1 package of the gelatin with 1 cup boiling water. Mix well, add 1 ice cube and stir. Set aside to cool.
2. Combine the ice, agave nectar, spiced rum, cinnamon and applesauce in a blender. Mix on medium speed until the ice is blended.
3. Stir in the triple sec and sweet and sour.
4. Stir in the gelatin. Mix well.
5. Pour the mixture into the molds or cups.
6. If you freeze in the cups, you can now sprinkle the top of the cups lightly with cinnamon and freeze.
7. Freeze for 45-60 minutes and add the wood sticks if using Liqoursicle molds.
8. Freeze overnight.

Serving

1. If you use a Liqoursicle mold, you can either let the mold sit out for 3-4 minutes or run some tepid water over the mold while making sure that the water flow is below the rim of the mold. Gently pull the sticks to remove. Sprinkle the molds lightly with cinnamon.

2. If you freeze the dessert in a cup, it is best served when removed from the freezer and allowed to thaw for 3-5 minutes. Enjoy!

Bob's Blasted Berry

Makes 4-6 Concoctions

These fresh berry flavored treats are like a frozen fruit salad with attitude!

Ingredients

3 ounces berry flavored vodka (See infused berry vodka page 14)

3 ounces raspberry puree*

3 ounces blueberry puree**

½ ounce fresh lemon juice

3 ice cubes

2 ½ teaspoons agave nectar

2 ounces Knox unflavored gelatin

Large sugar crystals - optional

* Raspberry puree- Blend 3 ounces of frozen (thawed) or fresh raspberries and 1 ounce water.

** Blueberry puree- Blend 3 ounces of frozen (thawed) or fresh blueberries and 1 ounce water.

Directions

1. Mix 1 package of the gelatin with 1 cup boiling water. Mix well, add 1 ice cube and stir. Set aside to cool.
2. Combine the ice, raspberry and blueberry puree, agave nectar, lemon juice and berry vodka in a blender. Mix on medium speed until the ice is blended.
3. Stir in the gelatin. Mix well.
4. Pour the mixture into the molds or cups.
5. If you freeze in the cups you can now sprinkle the top of the cups with the large sugar crystals.
6. Freeze for 45-60 minutes and add the wood sticks if using Liqoursicle molds.
7. Freeze overnight.

__Serving__

1. If you use a Liqoursicle mold, you can either let the mold sit out for 3-4 minutes or run some tepid water over the mold while making sure that the water flow is below the rim of the mold. Gently pull the sticks to remove. Sprinkle the molds lightly with the large sugar crystals.
2. If you freeze the dessert in a cup, it is best served when removed from the freezer and allowed to thaw for 3-5 minutes. Enjoy!

Buzz's Beyond a Cosmo
Makes 4-6 Concoctions

Infused berry vodka makes this Cosmo dessert sweet and sophisticated. The Sex and the City girls really missed out!!

Ingredients

1 ½ ounces berry flavored vodka (See infused berry vodka page 14)

1 ounce triple sec

2 teaspoons fresh squeezed lime juice

5 ounces cranberry juice

1 drop red food coloring

2 teaspoons agave nectar

2 ounces Knox unflavored gelatin

Large sugar crystals

Directions

1. Mix 1 package of the gelatin with 1 cup boiling water. Mix well, add 1 ice cube and stir. Set aside to cool.
2. Stir all of the ingredients except the gelatin into a pourable measuring cup or pitcher. Mix well.
3. Stir in the gelatin.
4. Pour the mixture into the molds or cups.
5. If you freeze in the cups you can now sprinkle the top of the cups with the large sugar crystals.
6. Freeze 45-60 minutes and add the wood sticks if you used a Liqoursicle mold.
7. Freeze overnight.

Serving

1. If you use a Liqoursicle mold, you can either let the mold sit out for 3-4 minutes or run some tepid water over the mold while making sure that the water flow is

below the rim of the mold. Gently pull the sticks to remove. Sprinkle the molds lightly with the large sugar crystals.

2. If you freeze the dessert in a cup, it is best served when removed from the freezer and allowed to thaw for 3-5 minutes. Enjoy!

Captain's Booty
Makes 4-6 Concoctions

Captain Morgan Rum gives a touch of spice to this tropical tasting treat!

Ingredients

2 ounces Captain Morgan Spiced Rum
½ ounce triple sec
6 ounces pineapple juice
½ ounce fresh squeezed lemon juice
2 tablespoons agave nectar
2 drops yellow food coloring
2 ounces Knox unflavored gelatin

Directions

1. Mix 1 package of the gelatin with 1 cup boiling water. Mix well, add 1 ice cube and stir. Set aside to cool.
2. Stir all of the ingredients except the gelatin into a pourable measuring cup or pitcher. Mix well.
3. Stir in the gelatin.
4. Pour the mixture into the molds or cups.
5. Freeze for 45-60 minutes and add the wood sticks if using Liqoursicle molds.
6. Freeze overnight.

Serving

1. If you use a Liqoursicle mold, you can either let the mold sit out for 3-4 minutes or run some tepid water over the mold while making sure that the water flow is below the rim of the mold. Gently pull the sticks to remove.
2. If you freeze the dessert in a cup, it is best served when removed from the freezer and allowed to thaw for 3-5 minutes. Enjoy!

Caribbean Casanova
Makes 4-6 Concoctions

You will be seduced by this creamy orange pleasing flavor.

Ingredients

2 ounces Malibu Coconut Rum

2 ounces orange vodka (see infused orange vodka page 18)

3 ounces cranberry juice

3 ounces orange juice

2 ounces Coco Lopez Coconut Cream

2 tablespoons agave nectar

6 drops yellow food coloring

2 drops red food coloring

2 ounces Knox unflavored gelatin

Directions

1. Mix 1 package of the gelatin with 1 cup boiling water. Mix well, add 1 ice cube and stir. Set aside to cool.
2. Stir all of the ingredients except the gelatin into a pourable measuring cup or pitcher. Mix well.
3. Stir in the gelatin.
4. Pour the mixture into the molds or cups.
5. Freeze for 45-60 minutes and add the wood sticks if using Liqoursicle molds.
6. Freeze overnight.

Serving

1. If you use a Liqoursicle mold, you can either let the mold sit out for 3-4 minutes or run some tepid water over the mold while making sure that the water flow is below the rim of the mold. Gently pull the sticks to remove.
2. If you freeze the dessert in a cup, it is best served when removed from the freezer and allowed to thaw for 3-5 minutes. Enjoy!

Caribbean Sunset
Makes 4-6 Concoctions

A sour tropical taste will put your mind in the Caribbean and your taste buds running back to the freezer to share these with friends.

Ingredients

1 ½ ounces Captain Morgan Spiced Rum

¼ ounce triple sec

3 ounces pineapple juice

½ ounce fresh squeezed lime juice

2 ounces fresh pineapple (approx 1 slice)

1 tablespoon agave nectar

2 ice cubes

1 ½ ounces Knox unflavored gelatin

Directions

1. Mix 1 package of the gelatin with 1 cup boiling water. Mix well, add 1 ice cube and stir. Set aside to cool.
2. Combine the ice, spiced rum, triple sec, fresh pineapple and agave nectar in the blender and mix on medium speed until the ice is blended.
3. Stir in the pineapple juice and lime juice. Mix well.
4. Stir in the gelatin.
5. Pour the mixture into the mold or cups.
6. Freeze for 45-60 minutes and add the wood sticks if using Liqoursicle molds.
7. Freeze overnight.

Serving

1. If you use a Liqoursicle mold, you can either let the mold sit out for 3-4 minutes or run some tepid water over the mold while making sure that the water flow is below the rim of the mold. Gently pull the sticks to remove.
2. If you freeze the dessert in a cup, it is best served when removed from the freezer and allowed to thaw for 3-5 minutes. Enjoy!

Dreaming of a Daiquiri
Makes 4-6 Concoctions

A great combination of tartness from the fresh lime juice, sweetness from the fresh fruit and fun from the rum!

Dreaming of a Daiquiri - Banana

1 ounce white rum

1 ounce banana liqueur

1 ripe banana

1 ounce fresh squeezed lime juice

1 tablespoon agave nectar

3 ice cubes

2 ounces Knox unflavored gelatin

Dreaming of a Daiquiri - Blueberry

1 ounce white rum

2 ½ ounces blueberry schnapps

5 ounces blueberry puree*

1 ounce fresh squeezed lime juice

2 ½ teaspoons agave nectar

3 ice cubes

2 ounces Knox unflavored gelatin

Large sugar crystals- optional

* Blueberry puree- Blend 5 ounces of frozen (thawed) or fresh blueberries and 1 ounce water.

Dreaming of a Daiquiri- Mango

1 ½ ounces mango infused rum or dark rum (see infused mango rum page 23)

½ ounce Cointreau Liqueur

5 ounces mango puree*
1 ½ ounces mango nectar
¾ ounce fresh squeezed lime juice
1 ½ tablespoons agave nectar
3 ice cubes
2 ounces Knox unflavored gelatin
Large sugar crystals

* Mango puree- Blend 5 ounces of frozen (thawed) or fresh peeled mango and 1 ounce water.

Dreaming of a Daiquiri- Orange

1 ounce white rum
½ ounce Cointreau Liqueur
1 ½ ounce fresh squeezed orange juice
3 ounces Mandarin orange puree*
½ ounce fresh squeezed lime juice
1 ½ tablespoons agave nectar
3 ice cubes
1 drop red food coloring
1 drop yellow food coloring
2 ounces Knox unflavored gelatin

* Mandarin orange puree - Blend 5 ounces of canned Mandarin oranges.

Dreaming of a Daiquiri- Peach

1 ounce white rum
1 ounce peach schnapps
1 ½ ounce peach nectar
4 ounces peach puree*
½ ounce fresh squeezed lime juice
2 ½ tablespoons agave nectar

4 ice cubes

2 ounces Knox unflavored gelatin

Large sugar crystals - optional

* Peach puree- Blend 4 ounces of frozen (thawed) or fresh peeled peaches and 1 ounce water.

Dreaming of a Daiquiri- Pineapple

2 ounces pineapple rum (See infused pineapple rum page 24)

2 ounces pineapple juice

5 ounces pineapple puree*

1 ounce fresh squeezed lime juice

2 teaspoons agave nectar

3 ice cubes

1 drop yellow food coloring

2 ounces Knox unflavored gelatin

Large sugar crystals- optional

* Pineapple puree - Blend 5 ounces of frozen (thawed) or fresh peeled, cored pineapple and 1 ounce water.

Dreaming of a Daiquiri- Raspberry

1 ounce white rum

1 ounce Chambord Raspberry Liqueur

5 ounces raspberry puree*

½ ounce fresh squeezed lime juice

1 ½ tablespoons agave nectar

3 ice cubes

2 ounces Knox unflavored gelatin

Large sugar crystals - optional

* Raspberry puree- Blend 5 ounces of frozen (thawed) or fresh raspberries and 1 ounce water.

Dreaming of a Daiquiri - Strawberry

1 ounce white rum

1 ounce Strawberry Liqueur- Fragoli is a good one

5 ounces strawberry puree*

¾ ounce fresh squeezed lime juice

1 ½ tablespoons agave nectar

3 ice cubes

2 ounces Knox unflavored gelatin

Large sugar crystals- optional

* Strawberry puree- Blend 5 ounces of frozen (thawed) or fresh strawberries and 1 ounce water.

Dreaming of a Daiquiri- Traditional Lime

1 ounce white rum

½ ounce triple sec

1 ounce fresh squeezed lime juice

1 ½ tablespoons agave nectar

3 ice cubes

2 ounces Knox unflavored gelatin

1 drop green food coloring- optional

Directions

1. Mix 1 package of the gelatin with 1 cup boiling water. Mix well, add 1 ice cube and stir. Set aside to cool.
2. Combine the alcohols, agave nectar, fruit purees, and ice in a blender and mix on medium speed. Mix until the ice is blended.
3. Stir in the juices. Do not blend or it will foam.
4. Stir in the gelatin.
5. Pour the mixture into the molds or cups.

6. Freeze for 45-60 minutes and add the wood sticks if using Liqoursicle molds. If you used the cups and would like your dessert sweeter, you can add the sugar crystals now once the tops are partially frozen.
7. Freeze overnight.

Serving

1. If you use a Liqoursicle mold, you can either let the mold sit out for 3-4 minutes or run some tepid water over the mold while making sure that the water flow is below the rim of the mold. Gently pull the sticks to remove. If you are adding sugar crystals to the desserts, you can now sprinkle the molds with the sugar.
2. If you freeze the dessert in a cup, it is best served when removed from the freezer and allowed to thaw for 3-5 minutes. Enjoy!

Easter Parade
Makes 4-6 Concoctions

You will have to fight the Easter Bunny for these tangy Easter desserts created with fruity sorbet and rum.

Ingredients

1 ¾ ounces white rum
1 ounce flat lemon-lime soda
1 scoop lemon sorbet (1/4 cup)
1 scoop orange sorbet (1/4 cup)
1 tablespoon agave nectar
3 drops yellow food coloring
2 ounces Knox unflavored gelatin
Large sugar crystals

Directions

1. Mix 1 package of the gelatin with 1 cup boiling water. Mix well, add 1 ice cube and stir. Set aside to cool.
2. Combine the rum, agave nectar, sorbet and food coloring in a blender and mix on low speed.
3. Stir in the flat lemon-lime soda.
4. Stir in the gelatin.
5. Pour the mixture into the molds or cups.
6. Freeze for 45-60 minutes and add the wood sticks if using Liqoursicle molds. If you used a cup you can now sprinkle the tops with the sugar crystals once they are partially frozen.
7. Freeze overnight.

<u>Serving</u>

1. If you use a Liqoursicle mold, you can either let the mold sit out for 3-4 minutes or run some tepid water over the mold while making sure that the water flow is below the rim of the mold. Gently pull the sticks to remove. If you are adding sugar crystals to the desserts, you can now sprinkle the molds with the sugar.

2. If you freeze the dessert in a cup, it is best served when removed from the freezer and allowed to thaw for 3-5 minutes. Enjoy!

Gorgeous Grape
Makes 6-8 Concoctions

Just looking at this dessert, with its generous amount of grape flavors, makes for mouth watering pleasure!

Ingredients

2 ounces grape schnapps
8 ounces Grape Kool-Aid*
4 ounces Grape Jell-O**
1 tablespoon agave nectar
1 ounce Knox unflavored gelatin

* Make the Grape Jell-O with 1 cup boiling water, mix well and add 2 ice cubes. Set aside to cool.

** Mix the Grape Kool-Aid with 3 cups of water and ¾ cup of sugar.

Directions

1. Mix 1 package of the gelatin with 1 cup boiling water. Mix well, add 1 ice cube and stir. Set aside to cool.
2. Stir all of the ingredients except the unflavored gelatin into a pourable measuring cup or pitcher. Mix well.
3. Stir in the unflavored gelatin.
4. Pour the mixture into the molds or cups.
5. Freeze for 45-60 minutes and add the wood sticks if using Liqoursicle molds.
6. Freeze overnight.

<u>Serving</u>

1. If you use a Liqoursicle mold, you can either let the mold sit out for 3-4 minutes or run some tepid water over the mold while making sure that the water flow is below the rim of the mold. Gently pull the sticks to remove.

2. If you freeze the dessert in a cup, it is best served when removed from the freezer and allowed to thaw for 3-5 minutes. Enjoy!

GORGEOUS GRAPE

GREEN SANDIA/MEXICAN FLAG

Green Sandia
Makes 4-6 Concoctions

A perfect addition to your Cinco de Mayo celebration! Turn on your Mariachi music and enjoy these bright green melon flavored Concoctions.

Ingredients

1 ounce white rum

3 ounces Midori Melon Liqueur

6 ounces pineapple juice

1 ½ tablespoons agave nectar

3 drops green food coloring

2 ounces Knox unflavored gelatin

Directions

1. Mix 1 package of the gelatin with 1 cup boiling water. Mix well, add 1 ice cube and stir. Set aside to cool.
2. Stir all of the ingredients except the gelatin into a pourable measuring cup or pitcher. Mix well.
3. Stir in the gelatin.
4. Pour the mixture into the molds or cups.
5. Freeze for 45-60 minutes and add the wood sticks if using Liqoursicle molds.
6. Freeze overnight.

Serving

1. If you use a Liqoursicle mold, you can either let the mold sit out for 3-4 minutes or run some tepid water over the mold while making sure that the water flow is below the rim of the mold. Gently pull the sticks to remove.
2. If you freeze the dessert in a cup, it is best served when removed from the freezer and allowed to thaw for 3-5 minutes. Enjoy!

Mexican Flag
Makes 8-10 Concoctions

Party and raise this decorative dessert to eat on Cinco de Mayo!

Ingredients
This recipe is a green, white and orange layered dessert.

GREEN- Green Sandia Recipe
1/2 ounce white rum

3 ounces pineapple juice

1 ½ ounces Midori Melon Liqueur

1 tablespoon agave nectar

2 drops green food coloring

1 ½ ounces Knox unflavored gelatin

White- Her Majesty's Sinful Colada Recipe
1 ½ ounces pineapple rum (see infused pineapple rum page 24)

1 ounce coconut water

1 ½ ounces pineapple juice

2 ounces Coco Lopez Coconut Cream

2 teaspoons powdered sugar

2 ounces Knox unflavored gelatin

3 ice cubes

Orange- Caribbean Casanova Recipe
1 ounce Malibu Coconut Rum

1 ounce orange vodka (see infused orange vodka page 18)

1 ½ ounces cranberry juice

1 ½ ounces orange juice

1 tablespoon agave nectar

3 drops yellow food coloring

1 drops red food coloring

1 ½ ounces Knox unflavored gelatin

Directions

1. Mix 1 package of the gelatin with 1 cup boiling water. Mix well, add 1 ice cube and stir. Set aside to cool.
2. **Green layer –** Stir all of the ingredients, except the gelatin, into a pourable measuring cup or pitcher. Mix well. Stir in the gelatin. Pour this mixture through a funnel into the molds or cups. By using a funnel the sides of the mold or cup will not get splashed with the mixture. Fill 1/3 of the cup or molds. Freeze for 45-55 minutes.
3. **White layer-** Combine all of the ice, Coco Lopez Coconut Cream, powdered sugar and coconut water in a blender and mix on medium speed. Stir in the pineapple juice and pineapple rum. Do not blend to prevent foaming. Stir in the gelatin.
4. Remove the molds or cups from the freezer. Make sure the top of the first layer is almost frozen. If you used a mold, put the wood stick into the mold of the green layer. You can now pour the white mixture through the funnel into the molds or cups. Fill the mold or cups an additional 1/3 on top of the green layer. Freeze again for 45-55 minutes.
5. **Orange layer-** Stir all of the ingredients, except the gelatin, into a pourable measuring cup or pitcher. Mix well. Add the gelatin and stir. You can now pour the orange mixture through a funnel on top of the white layer. Make sure the white layer is frozen enough to prevent the orange layer from penetrating it. You can tell by touching it lightly.
6. Freeze overnight.

Note: If your container of gelatin starts to thicken while waiting for each layer to freeze, you can put the gelatin container in the microwave for 10-15 seconds to melt it. It must be in liquid form to use.

<u>Serving</u>

1. If you use a Liqoursicle mold, you can either let the mold sit out for 3-4 minutes or run some tepid water over the mold while making sure that the water flow is below the rim of the mold. Gently pull the sticks to remove.
2. If you freeze the dessert in a cup, it is best served when removed from the freezer and allowed to thaw for 3-5 minutes. Enjoy!

Green with Envy
Makes 6-8 Concoctions

This tart lime treat will wake up your tongue to a mouth watering happy place.

Ingredients

1 ounce lime vodka (see infused lime vodka page 16)

2 ounces limeade - thawed if frozen

8 ounces lime sorbet - thawed

1 tablespoon agave nectar

2 ice cubes

1 drop green food coloring

2 ounces Knox unflavored gelatin

Directions

1. Mix 1 package of the gelatin with 1 cup boiling water. Mix well, add 1 ice cube and stir. Set aside to cool.
2. Combine the ice cubes, agave nectar, food color and vodka in a blender and mix on medium speed. Mix until the ice is blended.
3. Stir in the sorbet and limeade. Do not use the blender to prevent foaming.
4. Stir in the gelatin. Mix well.
5. Pour the mixture into the molds or cups.
6. Freeze for 45-60 minutes and add the wood sticks if using Liqoursicle molds.
7. Freeze overnight.

Serving

1. If you use a Liqoursicle mold, you can either let the mold sit out for 3-4 minutes or run some tepid water over the mold while making sure that the water flow is below the rim of the mold. Gently pull the sticks to remove.
2. If you freeze the dessert in a cup, it is best served when removed from the freezer and allowed to thaw for 3-5 minutes. Enjoy!

Island Breeze
Makes 6-8 Concoctions

You don't have to wait to escape to that relaxing tropical vacation spot; you can pamper yourself now by enjoying these exotic Concoctions.

Ingredients

3 ounces coconut rum

1 ounce pineapple vodka (see infused pineapple vodka page 19)

5 ounces pineapple juice

1 tablespoon agave nectar

1 teaspoon grenadine syrup

1 ounce coconut water

3 ounces Knox unflavored gelatin

Chopped drained pineapple - optional

Maraschino cherries - optional

Directions

1. Mix 1 package of the gelatin with 1 cup boiling water. Mix well, add 1 ice cube and stir. Set aside to cool.
2. Stir all of the ingredients except the gelatin, chopped pineapple and cherries in a pourable measuring cup or pitcher. Mix well.
3. Stir in the gelatin.
4. Pour the mixture into the molds or cups. You can now add a maraschino cherry and crushed pineapple to the inside of the mold.
5. Freeze for 45-60 minutes and add the wood sticks if using Liqoursicle molds.
6. If you used cups, let freeze 45-60 minutes before adding the cherries and pineapple to the top.
7. Freeze overnight.

<u>Serving</u>

1. If you use a Liqoursicle mold, you can either let the mold sit out for 3-4 minutes or run some tepid water over the mold while making sure that the water flow is below the rim of the mold. Gently pull the sticks to remove.
2. If you freeze the dessert in a cup, it is best served when removed from the freezer and allowed to thaw for 3-5 minutes. Enjoy!

Jameson & Cranberry, Jameson & Ginger Ale and Jameson & Lemonade

Makes 4-6 Concoctions

Even if you are not a whiskey lover, this full-bodied dessert will surprise you with how smooth and flavorful it is.

Ingredients

Jameson & Cranberry

1 ounce Jameson Irish whiskey

4 ½ ounces cranberry juice

½ teaspoon fresh squeezed lemon juice

2 teaspoons agave nectar

2 ice cubes

1 drop red food coloring

2 ounces Knox unflavored gelatin

Jameson & Ginger Ale

1 ounce Jameson Irish whiskey

4 ½ ounces flat ginger ale

2 ½ teaspoons agave nectar

2 ice cubes

2 ounces Knox unflavored gelatin

Jameson & Lemonade

1 ounce Jameson Irish whiskey

4 ½ ounces lemonade

2 ½ teaspoons agave nectar

2 ice cubes

1 drop yellow food coloring
2 ounces Knox unflavored gelatin

Directions

1. Mix 1 package of the gelatin with 1 cup boiling water. Mix well, add 1 ice cube and stir. Set aside to cool.
2. **Jameson & Cranberry** – Combine the ice, lemon juice, agave Nectar, whiskey and 1 ounce of the cranberry juice in a blender. Blend until the ice is liquid. Stir in the remaining cranberry juice and food coloring. Stir in the gelatin.
3. **Jameson & Ginger Ale** - Combine the ice, agave nectar, whiskey and 1 ounce of ginger ale in a blender. Blend until the ice is liquid. Stir in the remaining flat ginger Ale. Stir in the gelatin.
4. **Jameson & Lemonade** – Combine the ice, agave nectar, whiskey and 1 ounce of the lemonade in a blender. Blend until the ice is liquid. Stir in the remaining lemonade and food coloring. Stir in the gelatin.
5. Pour the mixture into the molds or cups.
6. Freeze for 45-60 minutes and add the wood sticks if using Liqoursicle molds.
7. Freeze overnight.

Serving

1. If you use a Liqoursicle mold, you can either let the mold sit out for 3-4 minutes or run some tepid water over the mold while making sure that the water flow is below the rim of the mold. Gently pull the sticks to remove.
2. If you freeze the dessert in a cup, it is best served when removed from the freezer and allowed to thaw for 3-5 minutes. Enjoy!

Jess's Pink Prescription
Makes 4-6 Concoctions

Beat the summer heat with this tart lemonade treat!

Ingredients

3 ounces vodka

6 ounces pink lemonade or crystal light

2 teaspoons agave nectar

2 ounces Knox unflavored gelatin

Directions

1. Mix 1 package of the gelatin with 1 cup boiling water. Mix well, add 1 ice cube and stir. Set aside to cool.
2. Stir all of the ingredients except the gelatin into a pourable measuring cup or pitcher. Mix well.
3. Stir in the gelatin.
4. Pour the mixture into the molds or cups.
5. Freeze for 45-60 minutes and add the wood sticks if using Liqoursicle molds.
6. Freeze overnight.

Serving

1. If you use a Liqoursicle mold, you can either let the mold sit out for 3-4 minutes or run some tepid water over the mold while making sure that the water flow is below the rim of the mold. Gently pull the sticks to remove.
2. If you freeze the dessert in a cup, it is best served when removed from the freezer and allowed to thaw for 3-5 minutes. Enjoy!

Jimbo's Jamaican
Makes 6-8 Concoctions

Ya' man! This sweet tropical rum treat will get your fun on! Crank up the Reggae Rasta music and party!

Ingredients

1 ounce Captain Morgan Spiced Rum

½ ounce Grand Marnier

1 ounce pineapple rum (see infused pineapple rum page 24)

2 ice cubes

2 tablespoons agave nectar

1 ounce grenadine syrup

2 ounces orange juice

6 ounces pineapple juice

3 ounces Knox unflavored gelatin

Crushed pineapple or pineapple slices - optional

Directions

1. Mix 1 package of the gelatin with 1 cup boiling water. Mix well, add 1 ice cube and stir. Set aside to cool.
2. Combine the ice, agave nectar, rum, Grand Marnier, and pineapple rum in a blender on medium speed. Mix until the ice is blended.
3. Stir in the orange juice, pineapple juice and grenadine syrup.
4. Stir in the gelatin.
5. Pour the mixture into the molds or cups. Add the crushed or sliced pineapple to the molds or cups.
6. Freeze for 45-60 minutes and add the wood sticks if using Liqoursicle molds. If you used cups, you can also add more pineapple to the top at this time. It should be frozen enough that the Pineapple will stay on the top.
7. Freeze overnight.

<u>Serving</u>

1. If you use a Liqoursicle mold, you can either let the mold sit out for 3-4 minutes or run some tepid water over the mold while making sure that the water flow is below the rim of the mold. Gently pull the sticks to remove.

2. If you freeze the dessert in a cup, it is best served when removed from the freezer and allowed to thaw for 3-5 minutes. Enjoy!

Kalena's Fiesta Sangria
Makes 8-10 Concoctions

Spanish wine and apricot brandy create an exotic-tasting fiesta perfect for a hot summer day! O'LE!!

Ingredients

12 ounces Spanish red wine (½ bottle - I used Monte Ducay Reserva)

2 ounces apricot brandy

2 ounces triple sec

2 ounces peach schnapps

4 tablespoons frozen lemonade concentrate, thawed

½ lime sliced

½ lemon sliced

½ orange sliced

4 ounces (8-10) Bing cherries, pitted and sliced

3 tablespoons agave nectar

5 ounces Knox unflavored gelatin

Directions

1. Mix all ingredients except the gelatin in a pitcher and refrigerate over night.
2. Make 1 package of the gelatin with 1 cup boiling water. Mix well, add 1 ice cube and stir. Set aside to cool.
3. Strain the mixture through a sieve into a bowl to remove all the fruit and sentiment.
4. Stir in the gelatin.
5. Pour the mixture into the molds or cups.
6. Freeze 45-60 minutes and add the wood sticks if using Liqoursicle molds.
7. Freeze overnight.

Serving

1. If you use a Liqoursicle mold, you can either let the mold sit out for 3-4 minutes or run some tepid water over the mold while making sure that the water flow is below the rim of the mold. Gently pull the sticks to remove.

2. If you freeze the dessert in a cup, it is best served when removed from the freezer and allowed to thaw for 3-5 minutes. Enjoy!

Long Day at the Office
Makes 6-8 Concoctions

Put up your feet and enjoy this scrumptious strawberry Concoction. It will help you mellow out after your workday!

Ingredients

1 ounce berry vodka (see infused berry vodka page 14)

1 ounce orange vodka (see infused orange vodka page 18)

1 ounce orange juice

1 ounce pineapple juice

4 ounces strawberry puree*

½ ounce grenadine syrup

1 ounce coconut water

1 tablespoon agave nectar

2 ounces Knox unflavored gelatin

* Strawberry puree - Blend 4 ounces of frozen (thawed) or fresh strawberries and 1 ounce water.

Directions

1. Mix 1 package of the gelatin with 1 cup boiling water. Mix well, add 1 ice cube and stir. Set aside to cool.
2. Stir all of the ingredients except the gelatin into a pourable measuring cup or pitcher. Mix well.
3. Stir in the gelatin.
4. Pour the mixture into the molds or cups.
5. Freeze for 45-60 minutes and add the wood sticks if using Liqoursicle molds.
6. Freeze overnight.

<u>Serving</u>

1. If you use a Liqoursicle mold, you can either let the mold sit out for 3-4 minutes or run some tepid water over the mold while making sure that the water flow is below the rim of the mold. Gently pull the sticks to remove.

2. If you freeze the dessert in a cup, it is best served when removed from the freezer and allowed to thaw for 3-5 minutes. Enjoy!

Luau Liftoff
Makes 4-6 Concoctions

Grab your flower Lei and coconut bra! After a few of these you will swear you hear Hawaiian music!

Ingredients

2 ½ ounces coconut rum

2 ounces pineapple juice

1 ounce cranberry Juice

2 ½ ounces pineapple puree*

1 teaspoon agave nectar

1 ½ ounces Knox unflavored gelatin

* Pineapple puree - Blend 2 ounces of frozen (thawed) or fresh sliced pineapple and 1 ounce water.

Directions
1. Mix 1 package of the gelatin with 1 cup boiling water. Mix well, add 1 ice cube and stir. Set aside to cool.
2. Stir all of the ingredients except the gelatin into a pourable measuring cup or pitcher. Mix well.
3. Stir in the gelatin.
4. Pour the mixture into the molds or cups.
5. Freeze 45-60 minutes and add the wood sticks if using Liqoursicle molds.
6. Freeze overnight.

Serving
1. If you use a Liqoursicle mold, you can either let the mold sit out for 3-4 minutes or run some tepid water over the mold while making sure that the water flow is below the rim of the mold. Gently pull the sticks to remove.
2. If you freeze the dessert in a cup, it is best served when removed from the freezer and allowed to thaw for 3-5 minutes. Enjoy!

Luck of the Irish
Makes 6-8 Concoctions

Top of the morning to you! The melon liqueur will have Leprechauns knocking on your door to enjoy these parties on a stick!

Ingredients

3 ounces peach schnapps

2 ounces Midori Melon Liqueur

2 ounces water

6 ounces orange juice

3 drops green food coloring

3 ounces Knox unflavored gelatin

Directions

1. Mix 1 package of the gelatin with 1 cup boiling water. Mix well, add 1 ice cube and stir. Set aside to cool.
2. Stir all of the ingredients except the gelatin into a pourable measuring cup or pitcher. Mix well.
3. Stir in the gelatin.
4. Pour the mixture into the molds or cups.
5. Freeze for 45-60 minutes and add the wood sticks if using Liqoursicle mold.
6. Freeze overnight.

Serving

1. If you use a Liqoursicle mold, you can either let the mold sit out for 3-4 minutes or run some tepid water over the mold while making sure that the water flow is below the rim of the mold. Gently pull the sticks to remove.
2. If you freeze the dessert in a cup, it is best served when removed from the freezer and allowed to thaw for 3-5 minutes. Enjoy!

Lucy's Lip Smacker
Makes 4-6 Concoctions

Fruit flavored liquors will make your mouth water and your lips dance for this pleasing Concoction.

Ingredients

1 ounce peach schnapps

1 ounce Mandarin orange vodka (see infused Mandarin orange vodka page 18)

½ ounce banana liqueur

1 ounce pineapple juice

1 ½ ounce grenadine syrup

2 ½ teaspoons agave nectar

4 ounces Mandarin orange puree*

2 ounces Knox unflavored gelatin

* Mandarin orange puree - Blend 4 ounces of canned Mandarin oranges and 1 ounce water.

Directions

1. Mix 1 package of the gelatin with 1 cup boiling water. Mix well, add 1 ice cube and stir. Set aside to cool.
2. Stir all of the ingredients except the gelatin into a pourable measuring cup or pitcher. Mix well.
3. Stir in the gelatin.
4. Pour the mixture into the molds or cups.
5. Freeze for 45 -60 minutes and add the wood sticks if using Liqoursicle molds.
6. Freeze overnight.

<u>Serving</u>

1. If you use a Liqoursicle mold, you can either let the mold sit out for 3-4 minutes or run some tepid water over the mold while making sure that the water flow is below the rim of the mold. Gently pull the sticks to remove.
2. If you freeze the dessert in a cup, it is best served when removed from the freezer and allowed to thaw for 3-5 minutes. Enjoy!

Ménage A Tois
Makes 6-8 Concoctions

This trio of liquors is a great blend of sweetness that will give your tongue a tantalizing treat!

Ingredients

3 ounces Midori Melon Liqueur

1 ounce peach schnapps

2 ounces pineapple vodka (see infused pineapple vodka page 19)

3 ounces pineapple puree*

4 teaspoons agave nectar

3 ounces Knox unflavored gelatin

* Pineapple puree - Blend 3 ounces frozen (thawed) pineapple or fresh sliced pineapple and 1 ounce water.

Directions

1. Mix 1 package of the gelatin with 1 cup boiling water. Mix well, add 1 ice cube and stir. Set aside to cool.
2. Stir all of the ingredients except the gelatin into a pourable measuring cup or pitcher. Mix well.
3. Stir in the gelatin.
4. Pour the mixture into the molds or cups.
5. Freeze for 45-60 minutes and add the wood sticks if using Liqoursicle molds.
6. Freeze overnight.

Serving

1. If you use a Liqoursicle mold, you can either let the mold sit out for 3-4 minutes or run some tepid water over the mold while making sure that the water flow is below the rim of the mold. Gently pull the sticks to remove.
2. If you freeze the dessert in a cup, it is best served when removed from the freezer and allowed to thaw for 3-5 minutes. Enjoy!

Mesmerizing Margarita's
Mango, Peach, Strawberry, Traditional
Makes 4-6 Concoctions

No lime sucking needed for these smooth tasting sweet and sour tequila creations.

Mesmerizing Margarita - Mango

1 ¼ ounces gold tequila

½ ounce triple sec

½ ounce margarita mix

½ ounce fresh squeezed lime juice

6 ounces mango puree*

2 ½ ounces mango nectar

2 tablespoons agave nectar

3 ice cubes

2 ounces Knox unflavored gelatin

* Mango puree - Blend 6 ounces of frozen (thawed) or fresh peeled mango and 1 ounce water.

Mesmerizing Margarita - Peach

1 ½ ounce gold tequila

½ ounce margarita mix

1 ½ ounces peach schnapps

½ ounce fresh squeezed lime juice

6 ounces peach puree*

2 ½ ounces peach nectar

2 tablespoons agave nectar

3 ice cubes

2 ounces Knox unflavored gelatin

* Peach puree - Blend 6 ounces of frozen (thawed) or fresh peeled peaches and 1 ounce water.

Mesmerizing Margarita- Strawberry

1 ¼ Ounce gold tequila

½ ounce margarita mix

¾ ounce strawberry liqueur - Fragoli is a good one

½ ounce fresh lime juice

6 ounces strawberry puree*

2 tablespoons agave nectar

3 ice cubes

2 ounces Knox unflavored gelatin

* Strawberry puree - Blend 6 ounces of frozen (thawed) or fresh strawberries and 1 ounce water.

Mesmerizing Margarita- Traditional

1 ounce gold tequila

¼ ounce triple sec

1 ounce margarita Mix

1 ½ ounces orange juice

½ ounce fresh lime juice

2 tablespoons agave nectar

3 ice cubes

2 ounces Knox unflavored gelatin

Directions

1. Mix 1 package of the gelatin with 1 cup boiling water. Mix well, add 1 ice cube and stir. Set aside to cool.
2. For all of the margarita recipes, combine the ingredients in a blender, except the gelatin and fruit juices, and mix on medium speed until the ice is blended.
3. Stir in the fruit juices. Do not blend to prevent foaming.
4. Stir in the gelatin.

5. Pour the mixture in the molds or cups.
6. Freeze for 45-60 minutes and add the wood sticks if using Liqoursicle molds. If using cocktail cups, you can sprinkle sugar crystals on the mango, peach or strawberry Concoctions.
7. Freeze overnight.

<u>Serving</u>

1. If you use a Liqoursicle mold, you can either let the mold sit out for 3-4 minutes or run some tepid water over the mold while making sure that the water flow is below the rim of the mold. Gently pull the sticks to remove. You can sprinkle the sugar crystals on the mango, peach and strawberry molds.
2. If you freeze the dessert in a cup, it is best served when removed from the freezer and allowed to thaw for 3-5 minutes. Enjoy!

Panty Raid
Makes 6-8 Concoctions

You can get your party on and enjoy the great blend of apricot flavor and sweetness even if you're in your big girl panties!!

Ingredients

2 ounces gold tequila

10 ounces (1 ¼ cup) apricot nectar

1 ounce fresh squeezed lime juice

3 tablespoons agave nectar

3 ounces apricot pie filling

2 ounces Knox unflavored gelatin

Directions

1. Mix 1 package of the gelatin with 1 cup boiling water. Mix well, add 1 ice cube and stir. Set aside to cool.
2. Stir all of the ingredients except the gelatin into a pourable measuring cup or pitcher. Mix well.
3. Stir in the gelatin.
4. Pour into the molds or cups.
5. Freeze for 45-60 minutes and add the wood sticks if using Liqoursicle molds.
6. Freeze overnight.

Serving

1. If you use a Liqoursicle mold, you can either let the mold sit out for 3-4 minutes or run some tepid water over the mold while making sure that the water flow is below the rim of the mold. Gently pull the sticks to remove.
2. If you freeze the dessert in a cup, it is best served when removed from the freezer and allowed to thaw for 3-5 minutes. Enjoy!

Papa's Paradise
Makes 6-8 Concoctions

A great addition to any summer party, this Concoction has a mellow mango taste that is as sweet and smooth as honey.

Ingredients

1 ounce white rum

2 ½ ounce mango rum (See infused mango rum page 23)

1 ½ ounce Midori Melon Liqueur

5 ounces mango puree*

6 ice cubes

1 tablespoon agave nectar

1 ounce pineapple juice

1 ounce orange juice

3 ounces Knox unflavored gelatin

* Mango puree - Blend 5 ounces of frozen (thawed) or fresh peeled mango and 1 ounce water.

Directions

1. Mix 1 package of the gelatin with 1 cup boiling water. Mix well, add 1 ice cube and stir. Set aside to cool.
2. Combine the ice, white rum, mango rum, Midori Liqueur, mango puree and agave nectar in a blender and mix on medium speed until the ice is blended.
3. Stir in the pineapple juice and orange juice.
4. Stir in the gelatin.
5. Pour the mixture into the molds or cups.
6. Freeze for 45-60 minutes and add the wood sticks if using Liqoursicle molds.
7. Freeze overnight.

<u>Serving</u>

1. If you use a Liqoursicle mold, you can either let the mold sit out for 3-4 minutes or run some tepid water over the mold while making sure that the water flow is below the rim of the mold. Gently pull the sticks to remove.

2. If you freeze the dessert in a cup, it is best served when removed from the freezer and allowed to thaw for 3-5 minutes. Enjoy!

Pink Coco
Makes 4-6 Concoctions

Coconut rum and pink lemonade make a finely textured yummy summer cooler!

Ingredients

3 ounces coconut rum

6 ounces pink lemonade

1 tablespoon agave nectar

1 tablespoon grenadine syrup

2 ounces Knox unflavored gelatin

Directions

1. Mix 1 package of the gelatin with 1 cup boiling water. Mix well, add 1 ice cube and stir. Set aside to cool.
2. Stir all of the ingredients except the gelatin into a pourable measuring cup or pitcher. Mix well.
3. Stir in the gelatin.
4. Pour the mixture into the molds or cups.
5. Freeze for 45-60 minutes and add the wood sticks using Liqoursicle molds.
6. Freeze overnight.

Serving

1. If you use a Liqoursicle mold, you can either let the mold sit out for 3-4 minutes or run some tepid water over the mold while making sure that the water flow is below the rim of the mold. Gently pull the sticks to remove.
2. If you freeze the dessert in a cup, it is best served when removed from the freezer and allowed to thaw for 3-5 minutes. Enjoy!

Pirates Brew
Makes 4-6 Concoctions

Ahoy Matey! A well balanced mix of fruit and brandy to keep any pirate cool.

Ingredients

½ ounce brandy

1 ounce Cointreau Liqueur

1 ounce peach schnapps

5 ounces pineapple juice

3 ½ ounces orange juice

2 tablespoons agave nectar

2 ounces Knox unflavored gelatin

Directions

1. Mix 1 package of the gelatin with 1 cup boiling water. Mix well, add 1 ice cube and stir. Set aside to cool.
2. Stir all of the ingredients except the gelatin into a pourable measuring cup or pitcher. Mix well.
3. Stir in the gelatin.
4. Pour the mixture into the molds or cups.
5. Freeze for 45-60 minutes and add the wood sticks if using Liqoursicle molds.
6. Freeze overnight.

Serving

1. If you use a Liqoursicle mold, you can either let the mold sit out for 3-4 minutes or run some tepid water over the mold while making sure that the water flow is below the rim of the mold. Gently pull the sticks to remove.
2. If you freeze the dessert in a cup, it is best served when removed from the freezer and allowed to thaw for 3-5 minutes. Enjoy!

Rainbow Rendezvous
Makes 6-8 Concoctions

With great pride, I created this multi-layered and fruit-flavored treat to enjoy with friends! It will take time and patience to make the colorful delicious layers but it's so worth the effort.

Ingredients

This recipe is a red, orange, yellow, green, turquoise, and purple layered dessert. It's best served as a Liqoursicle. If using cocktail cups, they will need to be large enough for all of the layers. You can also use one large clear glass bowl and serve it like ice cream.

RED

1 ounce white rum

1 ounce Fagoli Strawberry Liqueur or other brand

5 ounces strawberry puree

¾ ounce fresh squeezed lime juice

3 ice cubes

1 tablespoon agave nectar

1 drop red food coloring

2 ounces Knox unflavored gelatin

Orange

1 ounce white rum

½ ounce Cointreau Liqueur

1 ½ ounce fresh squeezed orange juice

½ ounce fresh squeezed lime juice

1 ½ tablespoon agave nectar

3 ice cubes

1 drop red food coloring

1 drop yellow food coloring

2 ounces Knox unflavored gelatin

Yellow

2 ounces pineapple rum (See infused pineapple rum page 24)

2 ounces pineapple juice

5 ounces pineapple puree

1 ounce fresh squeezed lime juice

2 teaspoon agave nectar

3 ice cubes

1 drop yellow food coloring

2 ounces Knox unflavored gelatin

Green

3 ounces peach schnapps

2 ounces Midori Melon Liqueur

2 ounces water

6 ounces orange juice

3 drops green food coloring

3 ounces Knox unflavored gelatin

Turquoise

1 ounce pineapple rum (see infused pineapple rum page 24)

½ ounce blue curacao

1 ounce Coco Lopez Coconut Cream

2 ounces pineapple juice

2 teaspoons agave nectar

2 ice cubes

1 ½ ounces Knox unflavored gelatin

Purple

2 ounces grape schnapps

8 ounces Grape Kool-Aid*

4 ounces Grape Jell-o**

1 tablespoon agave nectar

1 ounce Knox unflavored gelatin

* Make the Grape Jell-O with 1 cup boiling water. Mix well and add 2 ice cubes. Set aside to cool.

** Mix the Kool-Aid with 3 cups water and ¾ cup of sugar.

Directions

1. Mix 1 package of the gelatin with 1 cup boiling water. Mix well, add 1 ice cube and stir. Set aside to cool. You will have to make another gelatin mixture using the same directions while the yellow layer is freezing. Do not make both batches at once or it will gel before you can use it.

Note: If your container of gelatin starts to thicken while waiting for each layer to freeze, you can put the gelatin container in the microwave for 10-15 seconds to melt it. It must be in liquid form to use.

2. **Red layer -** Combine the alcohols, agave nectar, fruit purees, and ice in a blender and mix on medium speed. Mix until the ice is blended. Stir in the juices. Do not blend to prevent foaming. Stir in the gelatin. Pour 3 teaspoons of this color mixture through a funnel into ½ cup molds or cups. By using a funnel, the sides of the mold or cup will not get splashed with the mixture. Freeze for 25-35 minutes.

3. **Orange layer -** Combine the alcohols, agave nectar, fruit puree and ice in a blender and mix on medium speed. Mix until the ice is blended. Stir in the juices. Stir in the gelatin.

4. Remove the molds or cups from the freezer. Make sure the top of the first layer is almost frozen. If using molds, put the wood stick into the mold of the red layer. You can now pour 3 teaspoons of the orange mixture through the funnel on top of the red layer in the molds or cups. Freeze again for 25-35 minutes.

5. **Yellow layer -** Combine the alcohols, agave nectar, fruit puree and ice in a blender and mix on medium speed. Mix until the ice is blended. Stir in the juices. Stir in the gelatin. Remove the molds or cups from the freezer. Make sure the orange layer is almost frozen. You can now pour 3 teaspoons of the yellow layer through the funnel on top of the orange layer in the molds or cups. Freeze again for 25-35 minutes.

6. **<u>Green layer</u>** - Stir all of the ingredients except the gelatin into a pourable measuring cup or pitcher. Mix well. Stir in the gelatin. Remove the molds or cups from the freezer. Make sure the yellow layer is almost frozen. You can now pour 3 teaspoons of the green layer through a funnel on top of the yellow layer in the molds or cups. Freeze again for 25-35 minutes.

7. **<u>Turquoise Color</u>** - Combine the ice cubes, agave nectar and blue curacao and Coco Lopez Coconut Cream in a blender and mix until the ice is blended. Stir in the pineapple juice and pineapple rum. Stir in the gelatin. Remove the molds or cups from the freezer. Make sure the green layer is almost frozen. You can now pour 3 teaspoons of the turquoise layer through a funnel on top of the green layer in the molds or cups. Freeze again for 25-25 minutes.

8. **<u>Purple Layer</u>**- Stir all of the ingredients except the unflavored gelatin into a pourable measuring cup or pitcher and mix well. Stir in the gelatin. Remove the molds or cups from the freezer. Make sure the turquoise layer is almost frozen. You can now pour 3 teaspoons of the purple layer through a funnel on top of the turquoise color. Freeze overnight.

<u>Serving</u>

1. If you use a Liqoursicle mold, you can either let the mold sit out for 3-4 minutes or run some tepid water over the mold while making sure that the water flow is below the rim of the mold. Gently pull the sticks to remove.

2. If you freeze the dessert in a cup, it is best served when removed from the freezer and allowed to thaw for 3-5 minutes. Enjoy!

VOLUPTUOUS MELONS/WACKY WATERMELON

Raspberry Royalty
Makes 4-6 Concoctions

This lip-smacking raspberry liqueur creamy treat is the perfect Valentine for your loved one.

Ingredients

3 ounces Chambord Raspberry Liqueur

2 ounces pineapple rum (see infused pineapple rum page 24)

4 ounces pineapple juice

2 ounces Coco Lopez Coconut Cream

5 drops red food coloring

4 ice cubes

1 teaspoon agave nectar

3 ounces Knox unflavored gelatin

Directions

1. Mix 1 package of the gelatin with 1 cup boiling water. Mix well, add 1 ice cube and stir. Set aside to cool.
2. Combine the ice, agave nectar, food coloring, coconut cream and the pineapple rum in a blender and mix on medium speed. Mix until the ice is blended.
3. Stir in the Chambord and pineapple juice. Do not blend to prevent foaming.
4. Stir in the gelatin. Mix well.
5. Pour the mixture into the molds or cups.
6. Freeze for 45-60 minutes and add the wood sticks if using Liqoursicle molds.
7. Freeze overnight.

Serving

1. If you use a Liqoursicle mold, you can either let the mold sit out for 3-4 minutes or run some tepid water over the mold while making sure that the water flow is below the rim of the mold. Gently pull the sticks to remove.
2. If you freeze the dessert in a cup, it is best served when removed from the freezer and allowed to thaw for 3-5 minutes. Enjoy!

Ravishing Red Grapefruit Martini
Makes 4-6 Concoctions

Nothing bitter here, only an eye-opening sweet and juicy Concoction.

Ingredients

2 ounces red grapefruit vodka (see infused grapefruit vodka page 20)

4 ounces ruby red grapefruit juice

1 ounce Cointreau Liqueur

2 tablespoon agave nectar

2 ounces Knox unflavored gelatin

Large sugar crystals

Directions

1. Mix 1 package of the gelatin with 1 cup boiling water. Mix well, add 1 ice cube and stir. Set aside to cool.
2. Stir all of the ingredients except the gelatin and sugar crystals into a pourable measuring cup or pitcher. Mix well.
3. Stir in the gelatin.
4. Pour the mixture into the molds or cups.
5. Freeze for 45-60 minutes and add the wood sticks if using Liqoursicle molds. If you used cups, you can now sprinkle them with the sugar crystals.
6. Freeze overnight.

Serving

1. If you use a Liqoursicle mold, you can either let the mold sit out for 3-4 minutes or run some tepid water over the mold while making sure that the water flow is below the rim of the mold. Gently pull the sticks to remove. Sprinkle the molds with the large sugar crystals.
2. If you freeze the dessert in a cup, it is best served when removed from the freezer and allowed to thaw for 3-5 minutes. Enjoy!

Rockin Raspberry
Makes 4-6 Concoctions

Fresh raspberries and raspberry liqueur create a tempting sweet dessert.

Ingredients

3 ounces Chambord Raspberry Liqueur

8 ounces raspberry puree*

1 ounce fresh squeezed lemon juice

2 tablespoons agave nectar

5 ice cubes

2 ounces Knox unflavored gelatin

Large sugar crystals

* Raspberry puree - Blend 8 ounces of frozen (thawed) or fresh raspberries and 1 ounce water.

Directions

1. Mix 1 package of the gelatin with 1 cup boiling water. Mix well, add 1 ice cube and stir. Set aside to cool.
2. Combine the ice, agave nectar and raspberry puree in a blender and mix on medium speed. Mix until the ice is blended.
3. Stir in the raspberry liqueur and lemon juice. Mix well.
4. Stir in the gelatin.
5. Pour the mixture into the molds or cups.
6. Freeze for 45-60 minutes and add the wood sticks if using Liqoursicle molds. If you used cups, you can sprinkle them with the sugar crystals.
7. Freeze overnight.

<u>Serving</u>

1. If you use a Liqoursicle mold, you can either let the mold sit out for 3-4 minutes or run some tepid water over the mold while making sure that the water flow is below the rim of the mold. Gently pull the sticks to remove. Sprinkle the molds with the large sugar crystals.
2. If you freeze the dessert in a cup, it is best served when removed from the freezer and allowed to thaw for 3-5 minutes. Enjoy!

Ruby's Ringer
Makes 6-8 Concoctions

A great blend of citrus and sweet gives this grapefruit-flavored Concoction its flavorful punch.

Ingredients

2 ounces red grapefruit vodka (see infused grapefruit vodka page 20)

3 ounces ruby red grapefruit juice

6 ounces cranberry juice

8 ounces flat Squirt grapefruit soda

1 tablespoon agave nectar

2 ounces Knox unflavored gelatin

Directions

1. Mix 1 package of the gelatin with 1 cup boiling water. Mix well, add 1 ice cube and stir. Set aside to cool.
2. Stir all of the ingredients except the gelatin into a pourable measuring cup or pitcher. Mix well.
3. Stir in the gelatin.
4. Pour the mixture into the molds or cups.
5. Freeze for 45-60 minutes and add the wood sticks if using Liqoursicle molds.
6. Freeze overnight.

Serving

1. If you use a Liqoursicle mold, you can either let the mold sit out for 3-4 minutes or run some tepid water over the mold while making sure that the water flow is below the rim of the mold. Gently pull the sticks to remove.
2. If you freeze the dessert in a cup, it is best served when removed from the freezer and allowed to thaw for 3-5 minutes. Enjoy!

Rapturous Rum
Makes 4-6 Concoctions

Fruit juice, spiced rum and banana liqueur help you escape to your adventurous side.

Ingredients

3/4 ounce Captain Morgan Spiced Rum

1 ½ ounce banana liqueur

1 ounce pineapple juice

½ ounce orange juice

½ ounce grenadine syrup

3 ice cubes

1 tablespoon agave nectar

2 ounces Knox unflavored gelatin

Directions

1. Mix 1 package of the gelatin with 1 cup boiling water. Mix well, add 1 ice cube and stir. Set aside to cool.
2. Combine the ice, agave nectar, grenadine syrup and rum in a blender and mix on medium speed. Mix until the ice is blended.
3. Stir in the banana liqueur, pineapple juice and orange juice.
4. Stir in the gelatin. Mix well.
5. Pour the mixture into the molds our cups.
6. Freeze for 45-60 minutes and add the wood sticks if using Liqoursicle molds.
7. Freeze overnight.

Serving

1. If you use a Liqoursicle mold, you can either let the mold sit out for 3-4 minutes or run some tepid water over the mold while making sure that the water flow is below the rim of the mold. Gently pull the sticks to remove.
2. If you freeze the dessert in a cup, it is best served when removed from the freezer and allowed to thaw for 3-5 minutes. Enjoy!

Sarge's Salute
Makes 4-6 Concoctions

Your guests will be saluting your creative efforts for making these memorable strawberry-flavored Concoctions!

Ingredients

1 ounce coconut rum

1 ounce strawberry liqueur - Fragoli is a good one

1 ounce Coco Lopez Coconut Cream

2 ounces pineapple puree*

3 ounces strawberry Puree**

3 ice cubes

2 drops red food coloring

2 ounces Knox unflavored gelatin

* Pineapple puree - Blend 2 ounces of frozen (thawed) or fresh peeled pineapple and 1 ounce water.

** Strawberry puree - Blend 3 ounces of frozen (thawed) or fresh peeled strawberries and 1 ounce water.

Directions

1. Mix 1 package of the gelatin with 1 cup boiling water. Mix well, add 1 ice cube and stir. Set aside to cool.
2. Combine the ice cubes, Coco Lopez Coconut cream, pineapple puree, strawberry puree and food coloring in a blender and mix on medium speed. Mix until the ice is blended.
3. Stir in the coconut rum and strawberry liqueur.
4. Stir in the gelatin.
5. Pour the mixture into the molds or cups.

6. Freeze for 45-60 minutes and add the wood sticks if using Liqoursicle molds.
7. Freeze overnight.

Serving

1. If you use a Liqoursicle mold, you can either let the mold sit out for 3-4 minutes or run some tepid water over the mold while making sure that the water flow is the rim of the mold. Gently pull the sticks to remove.
2. If you freeze the dessert in a cup, it is best served when removed from the freezer and allowed to thaw for 3-5 minutes. Enjoy!

Southern Orgasm
Makes 4-6 Concoctions

You will be screaming over this eye-opening mix of peach schnapps, fresh peaches and Mandarin orange vodka!

Ingredients

1 ½ ounce peach schnapps

¾ ounce Mandarin orange vodka (see infused orange vodka page 18)

1 ounce triple sec

2 ounces orange juice

1 ounce peach nectar

4 ounces peach puree*

¼ teaspoon fresh squeezed lime juice

1 teaspoon agave nectar

2 ounces Knox unflavored gelatin

* Peach puree - Blend 4 ounces of frozen (thawed) or fresh peeled peaches and 1 ounce water.

Directions

1. Mix 1 package of the gelatin with 1 cup boiling water. Mix well, add 1 ice cube and stir. Set aside to cool.
2. Stir all of the ingredients except the gelatin into a pourable measuring cup or pitcher. Mix well.
3. Stir in the gelatin.
4. Pour the mixture into the molds or cups.
5. Freeze fro 45-60 minutes and add the wood sticks if using Liqoursicle molds.
6. Freeze overnight.

<u>Serving</u>

1. If you use a Liqoursicle mold, you can either let the mold sit out for 3-4 minutes or run some tepid water over the mold while making sure that the water flow is below the rim of the mold. Gently pull the sticks to remove.

2. If you freeze the dessert in a cup, it is best served when removed from the freezer and allowed to thaw for 3-5 minutes. Enjoy!

Spinner's Special
Makes 4-6 Concoctions

Squirt grapefruit soda makes this citrusy concoction very rejuvenating.

Ingredients

2 ½ ounces lemon vodka (see infused lemon vodka page 15)

6 ounces cranberry juice

5 ounces flat Squirt grapefruit soda

2 drops red food coloring

2 ounces Knox unflavored gelatin

Directions

1. Mix 1 package of the gelatin with 1 cup boiling water. Mix well, add 1 ice cube and stir. Set aside to cool.
2. Stir all of the ingredients except the gelatin into a pourable measuring cup or pitcher. Mix well.
3. Stir in the gelatin.
4. Pour the mixture into the molds or cups.
5. Freeze for 45-60 minutes and add the wood sticks if using Liqoursicle molds.
6. Freeze overnight.

Serving

1. If you use a Liqoursicle mold, you can either let the mold sit out for 3-4 minutes or run some tepid water over the mold while making sure that the water flow is below the rim of the mold. Gently pull the sticks to remove.
2. If you freeze the dessert in a cup, it is best served when removed from the freezer and allowed to thaw for 3-5 minutes. Enjoy!

Suntan Slinger
Makes 4-6 Concoctions

An appealing creamy mixture of coconut rum, banana liqueur and melon liqueur to help cool off on a hot summer day while getting your tan on!

Ingredients

1 ½ ounces cream de banana liqueur

1 ½ ounces coconut rum

1 ounce Midori Melon Liqueur

6 ounces pineapple juice

1 tablespoon agave nectar

2½ ounces Knox unflavored gelatin

Directions

1. Mix 1 package of the gelatin with 1 cup boiling water. Mix well, add 1 ice cube and stir. Set aside to cool.
2. Stir all of the ingredients except the gelatin into a pourable measuring cup or pitcher. Mix well.
3. Stir in the gelatin.
4. Pour the mixture into the molds or cups.
5. Freeze for 45-60 minutes and add the wood sticks if using Liqoursicle molds.
6. Freeze overnight.

Serving

1. If you use a Liqoursicle mold, you can either let the mold sit out for 3-4 minutes or run some tepid water over the mold while making sure that the water flow is below the rim of the mold. Gently pull the sticks to remove.
2. If you freeze the dessert in a cup, it is best served when removed from the freezer and allowed to thaw for 3-5 minutes. Enjoy!

Tea'd Off Arnold

Makes 4-6 Concoctions

A frozen concoction of that thirst-quenching summer drink of lemonade and sweet iced tea with a little something special added to it!

Ingredients

2 ounces lemon vodka (see infused lemon vodka page 15)

6 ounces sweet iced tea - can be found the refrigerated section at stores

5 ounces lemonade

2 teaspoons agave nectar

2 shakes ground ginger

2 ounces Knox unflavored gelatin

Directions

1. Mix 1 package of the gelatin with 1 cup boiling water. Mix well, add 1 ice cube and stir. Set aside to cool.
2. Stir all of the ingredients except the gelatin into a pourable measuring cup or pitcher. Mix well.
3. Stir in the gelatin.
4. Pour the mixture into the molds or cups.
5. Freeze for 45-60 minutes and add the wood sticks if using Liqoursicle molds.
6. Freeze overnight.

Serving

1. If you use a Liqoursicle mold, you can either let the mold sit out for 3-4 minutes or run some tepid water over the mold while making sure that the water flow is below the rim of the mold. Gently pull the sticks to remove.
2. If you freeze the dessert in a cup, it is best served when removed from the freezer and allowed to thaw for 3-5 minutes. Enjoy!

Titillating Tropical Tahitian
Makes 6-8 Concoctions

Pineapple juice and pineapple rum share the tropical flair of an exotic Tahiti vacation.

Ingredients

1 ounce dark rum

2 ½ ounces pineapple rum (see infused pineapple rum page 24)

½ ounce Cointreau Liqueur

3 ounces orange juice

6 ounces pineapple juice

6 ounces pineapple puree*

2 tablespoons agave nectar

2 ounces Knox unflavored gelatin

* Pineapple puree - Blend 6 ounces of frozen (thawed) or fresh peeled pineapple and 1 ounce water.

Directions

1. Mix 1 package of the gelatin with 1 cup boiling water. Mix well, add 1 ice cube and stir. Set aside to cool.
2. Stir all of the ingredients except the gelatin into a pourable measuring cup or pitcher. Mix well.
3. Stir in the gelatin.
4. Pour the mixture into the molds or cups.
5. Freeze for 45-60 minutes and add the wood sticks if using Liqoursicle molds.
6. Freeze overnight.

<u>Serving</u>

1. If you use a Liqoursicle mold, you can either let the mold sit out for 3-4 minutes or run some tepid water over the mold while making sure that the water flow is below the rim of the mold. Gently pull the sticks to remove.
2. If you freeze the dessert in a cup, it is best served when removed from the freezer and allowed to thaw for 3-5 minutes. Enjoy!

VOLUPTUOUS MELONS/WACKY WATERMELON

Voluptuous Melons
6-8 Concoctions

Fresh watermelon and peach schnapps blend to make this succulent summer refresher.

Ingredients

2 ounces peach schnapps

2 ounces watermelon schnapps

10 ounces watermelon puree*

2 ounces peach puree**

1 ounce fresh squeezed lemon juice

3 teaspoons agave nectar

3 ounces Knox unflavored gelatin

* Watermelon puree - Blend 10 ounces of fresh sliced, peeled, seedless, watermelon.

** Peach puree - Blend 2 ounces of frozen (thawed) or fresh peeled peaches and 1 ounce water.

Directions

1. Mix 1 package of the gelatin with 1 cup boiling water. Mix well, add 1 ice cube and stir. Set aside to cool.
2. Stir all of the ingredients except the gelatin into a pourable measuring cup or pitcher.
3. Stir in the gelatin.
4. Pour the mixture into the molds or cups.
5. Freeze for 45-60 minutes and add the wood sticks if using Liqoursicle molds.
6. Freeze overnight.

<u>Serving</u>

1. If you use a Liqoursicle mold, you can either let the mold sit out for 3-4 minutes or run some tepid water over the mold while making sure that the water flow is below the rim of the mold. Gently pull the sticks to remove.

2. If you freeze the dessert in a cup, it is best served when removed from the freezer and allowed to thaw for 3-5 minutes. Enjoy!

Wacky Watermelon
Makes 4-6 Concoctions

A mouth watering watermelon and tequila treat great for those summer BBQs!

Ingredients

1 ounces tequila

1 ½ ounces watermelon schnapps

¾ ounce fresh squeezed lime juice

5 ounces watermelon puree*

2 teaspoons agave nectar

2 ounce Knox unflavored gelatin

* Watermelon puree - Blend 5 ounces of fresh sliced peeled, seedless watermelon.

Directions

1. Mix 1 package of the gelatin with 1 cup boiling water. Mix well, add 1 ice cube and stir. Set aside to cool.
2. Stir all of the ingredients except the gelatin into a pourable measuring cup or pitcher. Mix well.
3. Stir in the gelatin.
4. Pour the mixture into the molds or cups.
5. Freeze for 45-60 minutes and add the wood sticks if using Liqoursicle molds.
6. Freeze overnight.

Serving

1. If you use a Liqoursicle mold, you can either let the mold sit out for 3-4 minutes or run some tepid water over the mold while making sure that the water flow is below the rim of the mold. Gently pull the sticks to remove.
2. If you freeze the dessert in a cup, it is best served when removed from the freezer and allowed to thaw for 3-5 minutes. Enjoy!

Kitchen Measures Conversion Tables (Approximate)

1 teaspoon		1/3 tablespoon
1 tablespoon	1/2 fluid Ounce	3 teaspoons
2 tablespoons	1 fluid ounce	1/8 cup
1/4 cup	2/3 fluid ounces	4 tablespoons
1/3 cup	2 2/3 fluid ounces	5 tablespoons & 1 teaspoon
1/2 cup	4 fluid ounces	8 tablespoons
2/3 cup	5 1/3 fluid ounces	10 tablespoons & 2 teaspoons
3/4 cup	6 fluid ounces	12 tablespoons
7/8 cup	7 fluid ounces	14 tablespoons
1 cup	8 fluid ounces	16 tablespoons
2 cups	16 fluid ounces	32 tablespoons
4 cups	32 fluid ounces	1 quart
1 pint	16 fluid ounces	32 tablespoons

INDEX

A

Aaliyah's Amazing   117
Alana's Almond   119
Andy's Twisted Trucker 124
Amaretto   46, 75, 119
American Flag   xv, 121-123
Angela's Apricot   126
Apple Cider   26, 107
Applesauce   107, 134
Apricot Brandy   126, 175
Apricot nectar   189
Apricot pie filling   126, 189
Arousing Almond   46

B

Banana   21, 47,83 113,133 145
Banana Hammock   47-48
Banana Liqueur   47, 109,
113,133,145,182,209,218
Banana Infused rum   21
Baileys Irish Cream   47,
49,51,66,77,86,95,101
Baileys Caramel Irish Cream   80, 107
Baileys Bombshell   49
Berry Pucker   130
Berry Infused vodka   14

Blackberry   14
Blast Off Banana   133
Blueberry   14
Blueberry puree 137,145
Blueberry schnapps   58, 145
Blue curacao   103, 121,133,199
Blushing Baked Apple   xv,134
Bob's Blasted Berry   137
Brandon's Cinnamon Cyclone xv, 26
Brandy   196
Buttered Buns   xiii,48-51
Butterscotch ice cream topping 51
Butterscotch schnapps 26,51,54
Buzz's Beyond a Cosmo 139

C

Candy Cane   xv,52
Captain's Booty 141
Captivating Caramel Tini 54
Caramel ice cream topping 54,80,107
Caribbean Casanova 142
Caribbean Sunset 143
Castries Peanut Cream Rum 61
Chambord Raspberry Liqueur 147,203,206
Champagne 26,28,31,35,37,41,43
Champagne Concoctions 25

Christmas Poinsettia xv, 28
Coco Lopez Coconut Cream 55.63,65.83,
103,109,.121.142.158.199,203, 211
Coconut Cupcake 55-56
Coconut water 55, 63,121,158,163.177
Cointreau Liqueur 124,
145,146,196,198,205,220
Cool Whip topping
46,49,59,69,75.89.93,101,111
Cranberry sauce 28
Cream Concoctions 45
Cream de Cacao 46,47,61,65,73,75,79,80,86
Cream de menthe liqueur 77,79
Cream of the Cropsicle 59
Cupid's Arrow Champagne xv, 31

D
Dolly Girl's Devil's Delight   xiii,61
Dreaming of a Daiquiri- Banana 145
Dreaming of a Daiquiri- Blueberry 145
Dreaming of a Daiquiri- Mango 145
Dreaming of a Daiquiri- Orange 146
Dreaming of a Daiquiri- Peach 146
Dreaming of a Daiquiri- Pineapple 147
Dreaming of a Daiquiri- Raspberry 147
Dreaming of a Daiquiri- Strawberry 148
Dreaming of a Daiquiri- Traditional 148

E
Easter Parade xv,151

F
Frangelico Hazelnut Liqueur 86
Fruit Concoctions 115

G
Ginger Ale 167
Godiva Chocolate Liqueur 61,73,83,97
Godiva White Chocolate Liqueur 52,73,111
Gorgeous Grape 153
Grape schnapps 153,199
Grand Marnier 171
Green Sandia xv,157
Green with Envy 161
Grenadine 117,163,171,177,182,195,209

H
Her Majesty's Sinful Colada   x111,63-64
Holiday Concoctions xv

I
Infused Alcohol 9-24
Introduction xvii
Island Hootch 65
Island Breeze 163

J
Jameson Irish Whiskey 167
Jameson & Cranberry 167-168
Jameson & Ginger Ale 167-168
Jameson & Lemonade 167-168

Jess's Pink Prescription 169

Jimbo's Jamaican 171

K

Kahlua Dream 66

Kahlua liqueur 65.,66,75,77,83,97,113

Kalena's Sangria 175

Ke Ke Key Lime Liqueur 69

Kinky Key Lime xiii,69-71

L

Laboratory 1-4

Lemon Infused vodka 15

Lemons 15

Lemonade 167,169,175,195,219

Lemoncillo liqueur 128

Lime Infused vodka 16

Limes 16

Long Day at the Office 177

Lori's Luscious Lemon 128

Luau Liftoff 179

Luck of the Irish xv,181

Lucy's Lip Smacker 182

M

Magical Moves Malted Milkshake 73

Mandarin Orange puree 43,146,182

Mango 17,23

Mango Infused rum 23

Mango Infused vodka 17

Mango nectar 146,185

Mango puree 145,185,191

Margarita mix 185,187

Marshmallow 75,93

Marshmallow Elf xv,75

Mesmerizing Margarita- Mango 185

Mesmerizing Margarita- Peach 185

Mesmerizing Margarita – Strawberry 187

Mesmerizing Margarita- Traditional 187

Measures 226

Ménage a Tois 184

Mexican Flag xv,158

Midori Melon Liqueur 35,109,113,157,158, 181184,191,199,218

Moaning Minty Chip 79

Minty Fudge Madness 77

Mocha Freeze 80

Molds 3

Monkey Business xiii,83

N

Nana's Nutella xiii,85

Nick the Nutty Nudist 86

Nutella Hazelnut Spread 85

O

Orange 18

Orange Infused vodka 18

P

Paddy's Shamrock xv,35

Panty Raid 189

Papa's Paradise 191
Passionate Peach Champagne xv,37
Peach nectar 37,89,146,185,213
Peach puree 37,89,146,185,213,223
Peach schnapps 89,117,146,175,181,182,184,
185,196,199,213,223
Peach Whip 89-90
Peanut Butter 61
Peppermint schnapps 52,223
Pineapple 19,24,143
Pineapple Infused vodka 19
Pineapple puree
130,147,179,184,198,211,220,
Pineapple Infused rum 24
Pink Coco 195
Pirates Brew 196
Pleasing Pistachio Cloud 93
Pomegranate Princess xv,41
Precarious Pumpkin Pie xv,95
Pumpkin cream liqueur 95
Pumpkin puree 95

Q
Queen B's Coconut Quest 97

R
Randy Russian 98
Rainbow Rendezvous 197-201
Rapturous Rum 209
Raspberry puree 130,137,147,206
Raspberry Royalty xv,203

Ravishing Red Grapefruit Martini 205
Red Grapefruit 20
Removing the molds 6
Rockin Raspberry 206
Root beer 101
Root beer schnapps 101
Ruby's Ringer 208
Ruby red grapefruit 20
Ruby red grapefruit juice 205,208
Rum
  Banana rum 21,47
  Coconut rum 55,97,142,158,163,179,195,
  211.218
  Dark rum 130,220
  Gold rum 23,24
  Light rum 21,130
  Mango rum 23,145,191
  Pineapple rum 24,63,93,103,121.147.158,
  171,191,198,199,220
  Spiced rum 134,141,143,171,209
  White rum 21,41,52,65,121,126,145,146,
  148,151,157,158,191,198

S
Sarge's Salute xv,211
Sassy Sassafras 101
Skinny Dipper xiii,103
Southern Orgasm 213
Spanish red wine 175
Spinners Special 217
Strawberry 14

Strawberry liqueur 31,121,148,187,198,211
Strawberry puree
31,121,148,177,187,198,211
Sticks 4
Sticky Caramel Apple xiii,107
Storing Concoctions 5-6
Suntan Slinger 218
Sweet & sour 119,134
Sweet iced tea 219

T
Tea'd Off Arnold 219
Tequila 185,187,189,225
The Morning After xv,43
Titillating Tropical Tahitian 220
Trade Winds 109
Triple Sec 97,134,139,141,143,148.175,185,
187,213

U
Unveiling your recipes 12

V
Vodka 14,15,16,17,18,19,20,117,169
  Apple vodka 107
  Berry Infused Vodka 14,137,139,177
  Lemon Infused Vodka 15,128,217,219
  Lime Infused Vodka 16,161
  Mango Vodka 17
  Marshmallow Vodka55,69,85,97.111
  Orange Infused Vodka
  18,124,142,158,177,182,184,213
  Pineapple Infused Vodka 19,163
  Pumpkin Vodka 95
  Red Grapefruit Vodka 20,205,208
  Vanilla Vodka 54,59,66
Voluptuous Melons 223

W
Wacky Watermelon 225
Watermelon puree 223,225
Watermelon schnapps 223,225
White Chocolate Bunny xv,111
Wicked Witches Brew xv,113

Made in the USA
San Bernardino, CA
12 March 2014